7ᵃ

Forever Foreigners or Honorary Whites?

Forever Foreigners or Honorary Whites?

The Asian Ethnic Experience Today

MIA TUAN

Rutgers University Press
New Brunswick, New Jersey, and London

Library of Congress Cataloging-in-Publication Data

Tuan, Mia, 1968–
      Forever foreigners or honorary whites? : the Asian ethnic
experience today / Mia Tuan.
            p.   cm.
      Includes biographical references (p.   ) and index.
      ISBN 0-8135-2623-X (cloth : alk. paper). — ISBN 0-8135-2624-8
(pbk. : alk. paper)
      1. Asian Americans—Cultural assimilation—Case studies. 2. Asian
Americans—Ethnic identity—Case studies. 3. Asian Americans—
Social conditions—Case studies. 4. Asian Americans—California.
5. Race discrimination—California. 6. Generations—California.
7. California—Ethnic relations.   I. Title.
E184.06T8 1999
305.895073—dc21   98-36388
                                                                                CIP

British Cataloging-in-Publication data for this book is available from the
British Library

The poem "The Ethnic Game" is reproduced by permission of the authors,
Nicole Kuwahara, Lee Lind, and Jonathan Reed.

Manufactured in the United States of America

CONTENTS

TABLES AND FIGURES

Tables

Figures

ACKNOWLEDGMENTS

Many people aided me with this project. While at U.C.L.A., I received excellent advice and mentorship from David Takeuchi, John Horton, Roger Waldinger, and Walter Allen. David and John, in particular, went beyond the call of duty in helping out a "lady in distress." Both shuttled me about campus and provided calm reassurance on a day when everything that could go wrong did go wrong. Also vital in keeping me sane that day were Marlies Dietrich, Desie Palad, Judy Greenberg, and Mary Jo Johnson. My special thanks to all of you.

Jeff Ow, Dominic Mah, Glenn Fukushima, Joy Yuson, Tram Mai Trinh, James Zhou, and Derek Mateo played major roles in helping me get the first shout-out to the wider community. Jeff, Dominic, and Glenn stuck around for some more fun with me and were joined by Albert Lowe back in the Bay Area.

Then there was a bizarre but meaningful detour to Iowa, about as far from the Asian ethnic experience as I could get. My wonderful colleagues at Grinnell College provided a generous fellowship that allowed for well-needed time and space to begin the writing process. From my Grinnell days, I would like to thank Mimi Bui, Yayoi Suzuki, Kent McLelland, and Chris Hunter.

Yen Espiritu provided excellent advice and continual encouragement during the latter phases of the project. I appreciate the energy and enthusiasm she has shared with me.

My parents, Winnie and Chang Chi Tuan, taught me the worth

of persistence and goal-setting, two values which served me well with this project. My humble and grateful thanks to them.

Lastly, I would like to specially acknowledge three people who have been instrumental mentors to me these last few years. Each crossed my path at crucial moments, bringing with them important lessons I needed to learn as well as the necessary and loving guidance to show me the way.

Larry Bobo profoundly influenced my intellectual and professional development. He has shown himself time and again to be a caring yet rigorous mentor whose belief in my abilities was unswerving. Larry has truly brought out the best in me, inspiring me during times of disappointment, encouraging me during moments of self-doubt, and otherwise pushing me to do my best work. His generosity has been without limits both at the professional and heart level. I walk away from graduate school with big shoes to fill; Larry has raised the bar pretty high as far as the type of mentor I will strive to be for my students.

Kesho Scott has taught me about matters of the heart and spirit, gently reminding me that a person can only hide in the safety of their head for so long before life's other lessons force you to look their way. Most importantly, she was there to catch me with steady and loving arms as my time to face these lessons arrived. I am eternally grateful for her wisdom, guidance, and friendship.

Michael Welch has and continues to offer the toughest lesson of all—that of creating a life in which independence and interdependence exist in harmony. It remains such a challenge for both of us to trust in the process. And yet, I feel that in this lifetime we may actually get it right. I couldn't ask for a better life partner.

Thank you for believing in me.

Forever Foreigners
or Honorary Whites?

THE ETHNIC GAME

Nicole Kuwahara, Lee Lind, and Jonathan Reed

The anticipation,
the excitement
of the exotic Far East
images of
dancing geisha dolls,
silk butterflies
are pictures he has of me.

He asks
"Where are you from?"

I say,
L.A.

"No, no, where are you *really* from?"
I'm from Torrance, if you want to go there.

He doesn't get it.
"Where are your parents from?"

Bainbridge Island.

"And, how about your grandparents?"

Ohh, my grandparents . . .
I calmly respond
well, they are from America too.

It has become an act of defiance
towards your ignorance
and assumptions.
That my Asian attributes could only mean
that I'm not from the same country you are.

You want to know where I'm from?
I'm from a land where Confucian principles rule,
But I'm also from a land where movie stars are made,
And where jets are built,
And where Mickey Mouse was born.

That's what I want you to know about me.

Introduction ▧ CHAPTER 1

In 1994, a Los Angeles judge attained international notoriety by being assigned to the "Media Event of the Century." As presider over the high-profile O. J. Simpson murder trial, Judge Lance Ito found himself unwittingly thrust into the limelight and the subject of intense public scrutiny. In the trial's early days few failed to tune into the unfolding drama. But as days dragged into months, observers grew increasingly restless as excitement surrounding Simpson's prosecution waned; the drama of real life was too slow-paced compared with what they were missing on preempted soap operas and talk shows. Judge Ito received his fair share of criticism for how the trial was proceeding. One incident involving New York Senator Alfonse D'Amato, however, stands out. While a guest on radio personality Don Imus's show, D'Amato expressed his impatience with the trial's pace by adopting a mock Asian accent and ridiculing the judge.¹ Ito, however, is a third-generation Japanese-American and speaks with no trace of a foreign accent. Ironically, like the judge, D'Amato is also a third-generation American whose grandparents immigrated to the U.S.

By most accounts Lance Ito is the picture of success, a man whose flourishing career began in 1975, shortly after he graduated from Berkeley's Boalt School of Law. In 1987, George Dukmejian, governor of California, appointed Ito municipal court judge, a plum opportunity for a twenty-seven-year-old prosecutor from the district attorney's office. Two years later, an even juicier plum came by way of an appointment to the Los Angeles County Superior Court, a prominent position that allowed him to showcase his talents and gain publicity. By forty-two, Ito had presided over the nationally observed securities fraud prosecution of Charles Keating, and the Los Angeles County Bar Association had named him trial judge of the year (1992), enviable achievements for someone so early in his career (Zia & Gall, 1995). The defining moment of Ito's professional life, however, will likely remain his involvement with the Simpson case, since relentless media coverage lasting well over a year indelibly etched his face and name into public memory. Today, Lance Ito is quite possibly the best-known jurist in the world.

Clearly, Ito is a man of professional accomplishment and international prominence. However, even a man of Ito's standing cannot escape racial and ethnic abuse. The indignities D'Amato subjected him to and the senator's chosen method for attack aptly symbolize the Achilles heel haunting many multigenerational Asian-Americans. Despite many Asian-Americans being longtime daughters and sons of this nation, some with lineages extending back to the 1800s, many people continually view and treat them as outsiders or foreigners within their own country. By choosing to speak in singsong pidgin, D'Amato took aim not only at Ito's professional performance but also at his ethnic and racial background (Kwoh & Su, 1995). D'Amato chose to see Ito not as a fellow American whose professional performance he was dissatisfied with, but as a caricatured foreigner he did not respect:

> *Judge Ito will never let it end. Judge Ito loves the limelight. He is making a disgrace of the judicial system. Little Judge Ito . . . will keep us from getting television for the next year.*[2]

▨ I chose to open with the Ito-D'Amato incident because it speaks directly to the questions that guide this book: (1) to what extent have multigenerational Asian-Americans (from now on called Asian ethnics), many of whom are well educated and living comfortable middle-class lifestyles, gained acceptance into the American mainstream, that is, have become seen as one of "us" instead of "them"? (2) as longtime Americans, how do Asian

ethnics identify themselves and what meaning(s) do they attach
to those identities? and (3) what are the roles of race and ethnicity
in their day-to-day lives? These were questions I was already pondering when news of
D'Amato's gaffe surfaced. Nevertheless, hearing how the senator
treated Ito caught me by surprise. Here was a third-generation
American, born and raised in the land of the Beach Boys, who
speaks little Japanese and is married to a white ethnic woman,[3]
and yet he was being mocked as a foreigner. The story resonated
with my own experiences as an Asian-American, but I wondered
if Asian ethnics related as well. Had they also experienced a tight-
ness in their guts, an odd mixture of anger, frustration, and sad-
ness upon hearing of the incident? Or was I, as a 1.5 generation
Asian-American, being too sensitive to this slight? Furthermore,
how did others make sense of this incident? Did they dismiss it
as a rare exception to the general rule of social acceptance, as the
action of an ignorant individual rather than anything more sys-
tematic? Or instead as a rare exception, might Asian ethnics have
viewed this episode as confirming some unwritten rule of conditional acceptance?

I started my research in this area with more than an academic
interest—the Ito-D'Amato incident glaringly confirmed how deeply
personal were the questions I was asking. I set off with renewed
determination to make sense of the experiences of a population
that I was both a member of and intellectually intrigued by.

From the outset I knew I wanted to explore what effect blatant forms of racism such as D'Amato's gaffe had on Asian ethnics'
sense of identity and comfort. But I was also aware of the need to
examine what Osajima (1993) calls the "hidden injuries of race,"
that is, the emotional costs accompanying subtler and yet
oftentimes more frequent experiences with racial marginalization.
In his work with Asian-American students and the impact of racism in their lives, Osajima (1993) poses the issue this way:

> [M]edia stories fail to tell us what it is like for students of color
> attending predominantly white colleges on those days when
> there seems to be no serious flare-ups. How does being a
> member of a visible racial minority affect a student's sense of

identity and belonging on the campus? To answer this question, we must move beyond a conceptualization of racism that focuses principally on overt manifestations of discrimination. Instead, we must delve beneath the surface to examine how racism affects the construction of students' everyday view of themselves and their actions on college campuses. (p. 82)

As a population that the media portrays as a "successful" minority, a "model" minority even, to delve beneath the surface of this image is particularly relevant. As Ron Wakabayashi, former director of the Japanese American Citizens League (JACL), aptly observes, "Asian Americans feel like we're a guest in someone else's house, that we can never really relax and put our feet up on the table" (Moore, 1988), a sentiment hidden beneath the glowing veneer of the model minority stereotype. Wakabayashi's words underscore the need to question the assumption that material success necessarily leads to social acceptance, a prominent feature within classic assimilation theory (Gordon, 1964). Yet, early scholars, with their biases toward studying white immigrants from Europe, never adequately addressed the role race might play in retarding or skewing assimilation processes.

From these early studies of white immigrants and their descendants, assimilation scholars such as Park (1950) and Gordon (1964) concluded that ethnicity's salience in people's lives declines with each passing generation. Today, identifying along ethnic lines or pursuing an ethnically embedded lifestyle has largely become an option for middle-class white ethnics (Alba, 1990, 1995; Alba & Chamlin, 1983; Bershtel & Graubard, 1992; Crispino, 1980; Gans, 1979; Kellogg, 1990; Lieberson, 1985; Phinney, 1990; Waters, 1990, 1992; Zenner, 1985). While in the not so distant past individuals worked, married, and socialized within ethnic boundaries with hardly a thought of doing otherwise, fewer are doing so now. As both the voluntary and involuntary reasons for maintaining strong ethnic loyalties including discrimination, residential segregation, self-isolation, and strong religious identification lessened, ethnicity's salience in people's lives declined and its nature changed. Even successive generation of immigrants from southern, central, and eastern Europe, once despised and seen as distinct and unassimilable races, have successfully merged with others of European ancestry and are seen today as Americans and members of a singular *white* race (Alba, 1985b; Allen, 1994; Hirschman, 1983; Ignatiev, 1995; Lieberson, 1981; Roediger, 1991; Steinberg, 1989). Today, white ethnics possess what Mary Waters (1990) has coined as a plethora of "ethnic options," the ability to choose whether or how ethnicity will matter in their lives.

Of course, acceptance did not take place overnight. European immigrants who poured into the country in the early part of the twentieth century suffered greatly at the hands of nativists who looked upon their cultures as backward and threatening to the American way of life (Higham, 1963). Nativists demanded that new-comers shed their language, rituals, and practices in exchange for an all-encompassing American identity and access to the privileges associated with that status. Clearly, these immigrants paid a heavy price, but the very success with which their descendants have be-come one of "us" has reinforced this country's belief in its ability to assimilate and embrace diverse peoples (Alba, 1995; Gordon, 1964; Park, 1950; Park & Burgess, 1921; Warner & Srole, 1945).

The question of the assimilation model's applicability to non–European Americans has been most sorely tested when applied to the black experience—in particular, the middle-class black expe-rience. Writings about the disillusionment and bitterness that the black middle class feels have exploded in recent years (Bell, 1992; Benjamin, 1991; Collins, 1997; Cose, 1993; Early, 1993; Feagin & Sikes, 1994; Fordham, 1996; Landry, 1987; Matusow, 1989; Powell, 1997; Robinson, 1998; Walton, 1989; West, 1993). Though many black Americans display visible signs of success, the main mes-sage captured in these studies is sobering: white America contin-ues to exclude and shun middle-class blacks, despite blacks' doing all the things (assimilating to white middle-class values and norms and accruing educational capital) they were told would bring so-cial acceptance. While the quality of their lives has improved ma-terially, race, contrary to the predictions of William Julius Wilson (1978), remains significant. Writer and filmmaker Anthony Walton (1989) poignantly captures this sentiment:

I like to think I lived up to my part of the bargain. I stayed in school and remained home many nights when I didn't have to in the interest of "staying out of trouble." I endured a lonely Catholic school education because public school wasn't good enough. At Notre Dame and Brown, I endured further isolation, and burned the midnight oil, as Dr. King had urged. I am sure I represent one of the best efforts that Americans, black Americans particularly, have made to live up to Dr. King's dream. I have a white education, a white accent, I conform to white middle-class standards in virtually every choice, from preferring Brooks Brothers oxford cloth to religiously clutching my gold cards as the tickets to the good life. I'm not really complaining about any of that. The world, even the white world, has been, if not good, then acceptable to me. But as I get older, I feel the world closing in. I feel that I failed to notice something, or that I've been deceived—I couldn't put my finger on it until I met Willie Horton.... Then one night, a temporary doorman at my Greenwich Village high-rise refused to let me pass.... Then a friend's landlord in Brooklyn asked if I was living in his apartment. We had been working on a screenplay under deadline, and I was there several days in a row. The landlord said she didn't mind, but the neighbors.... Then one day, I was late for the Metroliner, heading for Harvard and a weekend with several yuppie, buppie and guppie friends. I stood, in blazer and khakis, in front of the New York University Law School for 30 minutes, unable to get a cab. As it started to rain, I realized I was not going to get a cab.... As I cleaned up, I looked in the mirror. Wet, my military haircut looked slightly unkempt. My eyes were red from the water and stress. I couldn't help thinking, "If Willie got a haircut and cooled out . . . " If Willie Horton would become just a little middle-class, he would look like me. (p. 52)

Fordham (1996) speaks forcefully about the sense of disillusionment experienced by blacks such as Walton who make up the "crossover generation," those who came of age during the Civil Rights Movement and were the first to integrate into the white mainstream in mass numbers. Since ethnicity has long since faded as a salient marker for blacks, the issue of ethnic options is irrelevant. Instead, *racial options*, the ability to choose whether to identify or be identified along racial lines, stands as the key issue. Plainly, racial options have not materialized despite blacks' material success and longtime American status. Rather than becoming salient only if an individual black American chooses to "activate" that aspect of his or her identity, race remains an inescapable marker of difference that has consequences even for middle-class blacks. This understanding has led to profound disillusionment with the shortcomings of integration as well as a deep pessimism concerning the likelihood of ever being judged solely by their character rather than by superficial physical differences. Additionally, this realization has led to a closing of the ranks as middle-class blacks increasingly believe that black unity is more important than blending into the white world: "We as a people thought that integration was going to solve a lot of our problems, but the opposite is true" (Matusow, 1989, p. 153). The experiences of middle-class black Americans illustrate the need to understand how assim-ilation and acculturation processes operate for "racial-ized other" groups, those who fall outside the racial (read: white) norm.

Along this black-white continuum, where do the experiences of middle-class Asian ethnics, a *racialized ethnic* group for whom both racial and ethnic concerns are salient, fall? And how does the assimilation model fare in explaining questions of identity salience and belonging for them?

Surprisingly, a paucity of research regarding these questions is available. Further, the results of most of these studies conflict with one another. On one side are those who stress how far Asian-Americans have come in gaining acceptance. *"Oh, they've got no problems. What do they have to complain about?"* Variants of this sentiment can be heard from lofty academic circles to mundane lunchtime conversations. And the proof offered? News stories emphasizing Asian-Americans' apparent "takeover" of American higher education institutions; rising outmarriage rates along with low residential segregation patterns; and a rapidly growing professional middle class.

And yet, while I watched on national televison then-member

of Congress Norman Mineta, a third-generation Japanese-American, frustratingly ask for a little respect in response to D'Amato's antics, clearly, something was missing from these accounts: "I don't know what we, as Americans of Japanese ancestry, have to do to be able to prove that we are Americans" (Guillermo, 1995).

As racial minorities, Asian ethnics undoubtedly relate to some sentiments that middle-class blacks express. However, Asian-Americans have undergone *racialization* processes that are different from the processes that black Americans have experienced. That is, the ways in which whites have marked off Asians as "other" are not the same as those for blacks. For Asians, nativism and the stigma of foreignness further compounds racial marginalization. Blacks may be many things in the minds of whites, but foreign is not one of them. As far as racial positioning goes, Asians' designation as "model" minorities, the best of those in the "racial other" category, says it all—all "racialized other" groups are not equal in the eyes of whites.

Interestingly, some Asian-Americans have embraced the model minority label and see it as their ultimate ticket toward gaining social acceptance, while others reject the designation altogether. For example, far from feeling disillusioned, many students in Stacey Lee's study (1996) of Asian-American youth were convinced that with hard work, patience, and a little help from the model minority stereotype, they would someday gain the full approval of white Americans. They wrote off repeated incidents involving racism or discrimination as the acts of ignorant individuals, isolated experiences that they did not take seriously. What is important to note here, however, is that the students who adopted this strategy and believed that whites would eventually embrace them were immigrants. Native-born Asian-American students, on the other hand, were more likely to be suspicious of the model minority stereotype, to view racism as systemic, and to feel a sense of camaraderie and shared fate with other racial groups. As longtime Americans who struggled to be seen as such, they were skeptical that full social acceptance would ever be forthcoming.

So how are we to understand the Asian ethnic experience best? As more "white-like," more "black-like," or something altogether unique? What does it mean that Asian-Americans are considered the best of the "other" category? And how does this label affect their sense of identity and belonging? More important, what can their experiences tell us about the different positionings of racial groups in the United States?

I knew the answers to these questions did not lay in available survey and census data, but emerge from in-depth and personal conversations with Asian ethnics. My interest was not in questioning whether Asian ethnics have made material gains, but in exploring if these gains have yielded social acceptance, that is, have allowed for an abundance of ethnic as well as racial options. To the extent they had not, I believed, would necessitate revising existing theoretical work on ethnic salience for later generation Americans and looking beneath the exterior of the model minority image.

To pursue these questions, I led a research team in locating and interviewing middle-class Asian ethnics residing in California.[4] Between 1994 and 1995 we hit the streets of Los Angeles and the San Francisco peninsula, areas known for their long-standing Asian-American communities, in search of third-generation and later Chinese- and Japanese-Americans who were willing to share their experiences, opinions, and concerns.

Using the snowball sample technique, we spoke with ninety-five Asian ethnics, with roughly equal proportions of each sex and ethnicity and ranging in age from their early twenties to late seventies (see Appendix B for a complete list). The majority are white-collar professionals in fields such as medicine/health, banking, law, engineering, publishing, computer technology, education, finance, insurance, and real estate. Additional respondents included homemakers, small business owners, students, and a few artists.

We conducted interviews wherever convenient for our informants: in their homes, at cafes and restaurants, at work, and occasionally at my University of California at Los Angeles (U.C.L.A.) office; each session ranged from one to three hours and was tape recorded. The interviews covered five general areas: (1) early memories and experiences with Chinese/Japanese culture; (2) current lifestyle and ethnic practices; (3) ethnic identity issues; (4) experiences with racism and discrimination; and (5) attitudes toward current Asian immigration and also the social status of Asian-Americans today (see Appendix A for the questionnaire). To stimulate thoughtful reflection rather than a quick response, most of the questions were open-ended.

One of the main concerns with snowball sampling is that of network bias, the tendency of respondents to refer the researcher to "like-minded" individuals. To offset this tendency, we tried to begin with as many independent informants as possible. The number of researchers on the team (eight, including myself) helped diversify our starting points. Referrals from several ethnic organizations, word of mouth, chance encounters, and acquaintances provided the bulk of our initial informants; after that, we contacted people whom our interviewees referred to us. In a handful of cases, we interviewed the siblings, spouses, and adult children of respondents to explore similarities and differences within a family unit.

▨ *Studying Chinese and Japanese Ethnics*

I decided to limit the study to only Chinese and Japanese ethnics for a variety of reasons. As two of the oldest and most established Asian ethnic groups, I knew that locating potential participants who were at least third generation would not be difficult. Also, studying two groups allowed for a comparison of post-immigration culture and history. Further, we could explore how their unique experiences affected their racial and ethnic identities. Some scholars (Fugita & O'Brien, 1991a; Kendis, 1989) argue that sociohistorical factors unique to Japanese-Americans have led them to maintain salient ethnic identities simultaneous to assimilating at the structural level. Therefore, while the content of the culture may have changed, the tendency to associate with coethnics and desire to maintain a cohesive community persists. Lyman (1986), in contrast, argues the reverse—while Japanese-Americans have extensively integrated into the American mainstream, the Chinese are the ones who have maintained salient ethnic ties. Such discrepancies in findings call for a reconsideration of ethnic differences among Asian subgroups.

Along with proposed cultural differences in ethnic affinity, different histories of settlement and reception in the United States that may affect ethnic salience mark the two groups. These include differences in initial community structure as well as degree of persecution experienced here.

Differences in Initial Community Structure

The Chinese were the first Asians to immigrate to America in significant numbers. The vast majority began arriving around the 1850s and these "sojourners" were men who dreamed of making quick fortunes and returning home wealthy (Kitano & Daniels, 1995; Takaki, 1989b; Wong, 1995). However, as the reality of circumscribed employment opportunities and racial discrimination set in, these dreams gradually faded. Chinese migrants soon discovered that the work open to them was primarily as miners, manufacture workers, and laborers (Chan, 1991b; Daniels, 1972, 1988). In addition, they found themselves subject to unfair taxation, licensing, duties, fines, and other legislation aimed at discouraging permanent settlement and economic success. For example, as Chinese miners became an economic threat to white miners, the California legislature enacted a foreign miners' tax requiring all foreign-born and nonnaturalized citizens to pay a monthly license (Daniels, 1988; Hing, 1993). Since the Chinese were ineligible for citizenship based on a 1789 federal statute limiting naturalization to "free white persons," they found themselves in a precarious position. Similarly, legislation calling for a $50 tax on each Chinese passenger who arrived by ship and was *ineligible for citizenship* left them with no recourse but to pay the tax.

Hostilities toward the Chinese grew as their numbers increased. White workers continued to see Chinese laborers as economic competitors, a situation that prompted further legislation to restrict their occupational pursuits and economic potential (Daniels, 1988; Hing, 1993; U.S. Commission on Civil Rights, 1986). This resentment culminated in the Chinese Exclusion Act of 1882.

The act suspended further immigration of all Chinese laborers to the United States for 10 years, and it prohibited all persons of Chinese ancestry already residing here from obtaining

United States citizenship after the effective date of the act. An 1888 amendment applied the exclusion to all Chinese except officials, merchants, students, teachers, and tourists. At the time of the Chinese Exclusion Act, approximately 105,000 persons of Chinese descent lived in the United States, 100,000 of whom were male. Although some concern was expressed about the harshness of continuing exclusion, the Chinese Exclusion Act was extended for 10 years in 1892, for 2 years in 1902, and indefinitely in 1904. (U.S. Commission on Civil Rights, 1986, p. 8)

Perhaps the most significant consequence of the Chinese Exclusion Act was its effect on the future demographic profile of the Chinese-American community. While some merchants, diplomats, and clergymen brought their families with them, most male sojourners did not intend to remain in the United States. However, even if they had decided to stay, they lacked resources to support families here. The men who emigrated were expected to leave their wives and children with family in China to guarantee that they would send remittances and return home (Chan, 1991a; Nee & Wong, 1985; Takaki, 1989b). With passage of the Chinese Exclusion Act, a life of forced "bachelorhood" awaited many men already living in the United States—they had not earned enough money to return home comfortably, and the act did not allow them to send for their wives. Also, racist legislation constantly changed the rules and left most Chinese with no recourse but to stay put lest they be barred from reentering. A few found ways, both legal and extralegal, to circumvent immigration restrictions and bring in their wives; the majority did not. The outcome was an enormous imbalance in the ratio of Chinese men to women; in 1890 there were twenty-seven Chinese men for every Chinese woman (Hing, 1993; Wong, 1995). Such a woefully unbalanced sex ratio severely hindered the population growth of native-born Chinese for generations, thus delaying normal community development for years (Chan, 1991a; Wong, 1995). The Chinese ethnics interviewed in this study are the descendants of the lucky few who successfully brought, smuggled, or started families in the United States.

The Japanese, ironically, began immigrating to the United

States shortly after passage of the Chinese Exclusion Act and were brought in partly as replacements for outgoing Chinese laborers in California (Fugita & O'Brien, 1991b; Nee & Sanders, 1985). Similar to their Chinese counterparts, the Japanese faced limited employment opportunities; racist trade unions closed many manufacturing jobs to them. Therefore, they turned to agriculture, fishing, and small businesses that catered to the needs of other Japanese (Daniels, 1972). Because of the intensive farming techniques that they had brought from their homeland, their role in developing and cultivating California's agriculture is of particular significance. According to Daniels (1972), by 1910 the Japanese produced approximately 10 percent of the dollar volume of California's crops while owning a mere 1 percent of the state's land under cultivation.

With statistics such as these, it comes as no surprise that Japanese farmers quickly became subjects of concern. White farmers saw them as dangerous economic competitors and demanded protection from their California legislators (Fugita & O'Brien, 1991b). They feared that Japanese "hordes" were invading California and taking over the state (Daniels, 1972), sentiments that would re-emerge in the 1980s with Japanese buying real estate in California. These early lawmakers responded by passing the Alien Land Law in 1913, barring foreign-born Japanese from owning property (Hing, 1993). Loopholes, however, enabled the Japanese to circumvent the law with sharecropping and leasing programs until a tougher version of the law was passed in 1920.

In contrast to the Chinese, early Japanese settlers were more likely to come as intact families or as single men who later sent for their families (Daniels, 1988; Hing, 1993; Kendis, 1989; Lyman, 1986; Takaki, 1989b). In explaining this difference, Nee and Sanders (1985) argue that the social structure of nineteenth- and early twentieth-century Japanese rural life encouraged sons who were not the firstborn to pursue their fortunes elsewhere. Japanese immigrants did not experience cultural sanctions for bringing their families with them to America; the Japanese government encouraged them to do so (Hing, 1993; Takaki, 1989b). Moreover, Japan was in a much better position to make demands on the government of the United States to allow for family reunification, owing to its political power and military strength; China, on the other hand, weak from internal strife and civil war, had little with which to bargain (Daniels, 1972). Subsequently, early Japanese settlers successfully established families and communities and, by extension, planted the seeds for future generations of Japanese ethnics. Today, significant third-, fourth-, and even fifth-generation Japanese-American populations reflect this history. Chinese-Americans, in contrast, while numerically greater than the Japanese, have a smaller proportion of third-generation and later ethnics. Furthermore, the Chinese, while historically the older of the two groups, have immigrated in significant numbers since passage of the 1965 Immigration Act, the landmark legislation responsible for reinvigorating Asian immigration. The Japanese, in contrast, have only experienced a moderate amount of immigration in recent years. Therefore, the proportion of foreign-born to native-born is much higher for Chinese than for Japanese.

Japanese-American Internment

We believe that when we are dealing with the Caucasian race we have methods that will test the loyalty of them, and we believe that we can in dealing with the Germans and Italians, arrive at some fairly sound conclusions because of our knowledge of the way they live in the community and have lived for many years. But when we deal with the Japanese, we are in an entirely different field, and we cannot form any opinion that we believe to be sound. Their methods of living, language, make for this difficulty. (Earl Warren, California State Attorney General, soon to be governor of California and eventually chief justice of the United States Supreme Court, quote in Goldberg, 1970, pp. 97–98).

Another factor distinguishing the Japanese-American experience from the Chinese-American experience stems from the former's forced evacuation and internment during World War II. On February 19, 1942, President Franklin D. Roosevelt signed Executive Order 9066, authorizing Secretary of War Henry Stimson to remove any U.S. citizens and/or aliens from designated areas for national security. Officially, all descendants of Axis nations living along the west coast were subjects of concern, but as illustrated in the above passage, the Japanese were really the ones in question. Their "foreignness," based on perceived racial and cultural differences, cleared the way for the unique treatment they received. Faced with mounting fears over possible sabotage and espionage, orders were given for the removal of more than 110,000 Japanese-Americans, two-thirds of whom were American-born citizens, from the states of California, Oregon, Washington, and Arizona (Daniels, 1972; Nagata, 1993).

In the days following the evacuation order, chaos reigned. Without any firm idea of where they would go, how long they would be gone, or what they needed to bring, community members prepared for an unknown journey. They had to decide what to do with personal and business property (homes/farms, furniture, equipment, etc.) as well as arrange other aspects of daily living, usually with only a few days' notice. (Community on Wartime Relocation and Internment of Civilians [CWRIC], 1982; Daniels, 1972, 1991; Kitano, 1992). In short, their lives were turned upside down; personal control was completely wrested from them, and they could do nothing about it.

Initially, they were sent to temporary relocation centers, usually found in converted racetracks or fairgrounds, where they got their first taste of what life was to be like for the next few years: communal barracks, dining halls, and bathing facilities. From there, these people were eventually moved to one of ten permanent "camps," complete with barbed-wire fences, watch towers, and armed guards. For many, this would serve as home for the next few years.

That all Japanese, irrespective of generation, were singled out for "looking like the enemy" while German-Americans and Italian-Americans were not, aptly captures the significant role race prejudice played (Daniels, 1972, 1988; Nagata, 1993). Instead, they were viewed as an undifferentiated collective, with guilt meted out accordingly (Daniels, 1988). From military leaders to the mass media, virtually all were unwilling to view Japanese as individuals and decide guilt or innocence accordingly—"A Jap's a Jap"—was a common sentiment expressed at the time.

Native-born Americans of German or Italian ancestry were treated differently; their innocence was assumed until proven otherwise (Daniels, 1972). Of the German and Italian citizens who were officially classified as "enemy aliens" after World War II began, only a small fraction were actually interned. In addition, as the opening passage illustrates, America's bias toward and familiarity with European immigrants was a reality (Higham, 1963). If anything, the war aided the assimilation of German- and Italian-Americans. As Alba (1985b) argues, World War II had the powerful effect of shifting ethnic identity into national loyalty, thereby encouraging Italians to think of themselves as Americans and, in turn, to be seen as legitimate Americans. Lieberson (1985) similarly points to the importance of the war in hastening the assimilation process for German-Americans, noting the sharp decline in the number of people identifying as German during the war. Some avoided social persecution by changing their names, forgoing their German ancestry, and slipping unobtrusively into the American mainstream.

Japanese-Americans, in contrast, could not "pass" into the American mainstream, nor were they allowed to prove their allegiance to the United States. Their high visibility, small numbers, and lack of political power left them defenseless to fight against the wartime hysteria and race prejudice that resulted in their internment.

Clearly, the history of Japanese-Americans in this society is indelibly marked by their wartime internment. With the emergence of camp anniversaries, reunions, and pilgrimages, internment has become a potent symbol for generating ethnic solidarity much as the Holocaust is for Jewish-Americans (Fugita & O'Brien, 1991b; Nagata, 1993). The redress movement, for example, has awakened lines of communication within many Japanese-American families and ethnic communities. This aspect of their group experience sets them apart from Chinese ethnics and may play a significant role in promoting a salient ethnic identity even among current generations with no direct internment experience.

▧ California, The Symbolic Capital of Asian America

Ever since Chinese laborers were first brought to labor in mines and on railroad tracks, California has remained the state with the largest concentration of Asian-Americans (Barringer, Gardner, & Levin, 1993; Min, 1995). According to 1990 Census figures, approximately 40 percent of the nation's Asian-Americans reside in California; New York is a distant 10 percent (Barringer et al., 1993). California is also a particularly appropriate place for studying native-born Chinese- and Japanese-Americans; 42 percent of the nation's native-born Chinese and 36 percent of native-born Japanese reside there.

Clearly, California is a rich and essential site for studying the Asian-American experience. Strangely though, whether their numbers and long history have promoted greater social acceptance or the reverse—greater hostility—is not at all clear.

In theory, the concentration of Asian-Americans in California may give rise to discrimination from whites who perceive themselves to be threatened economically (or otherwise) by large groups of "outsiders." On the other hand, it is plausible that the relatively large numbers of Asian-Americans in California may contribute to lower levels of discrimination due to increased contact and interaction between whites and Asians (Nee & Sanders, 1985, p. 79).

Asian ethnics in California have the most substantive reasons to feel part of the mainstream and subsequently to feel that ethnicity is an optional part of their identity. After all, they have been present in the state since the mid 1800s, are well integrated into its social fabric, and may be found in all occupational fields. Further, California is the primary receiving state for Asian immigrants, a situation that may actually reinforce a sense of ethnic identity among Asian ethnics. Immigrants breathe new life into ethnic communities by providing fresh reminders of ethnic cultures and practices. Asian ethnics may find themselves participating more often in ethnic activities in response to the increased availability of Asian groceries and stores, cultural celebrations, educational programs, and restaurants (Min, 1995b).

In addition, the general climate toward immigrants, both legal and illegal, is decidedly less hospitable today. With California's governor Pete Wilson leading the way to eliminate all social service programs for illegal immigrants and curtail many benefits offered to legal immigrants, increased hostilities come as no surprise. Asian ethnics who are mistaken for Asian immigrants have received some of this negativity (Horton, 1995; Noble, 1995; Saito, 1993). Possibly, such cases of mistaken identity may cause Asian ethnics to question their own levels of acceptance by the mainstream. Subsequently, because of perceived social exclusion, ethnicity may become more salient for them.

▨ *Direction and Scope of the Study*

In the pages to follow, I discuss the personal meanings and salience our respondents attach to their ethnic identities and compare these observations with what has been found to be the case for white ethnics. I examine the ways ethnicity matters in their lives and the ways it does not. Second, I explore the role Asian-Americans, as a whole, play in national discussions about race.

In brief, I argue that ethnicity's role in my informants' lives has changed in much the same ways it has for middle-class white ethnics. They exercise a great deal of choice regarding the ethnic practices and values they wish to integrate or discard from their *personal lives*. Nevertheless, ethnicity is far from an optional facet of their *public lives* because others continue to define them in racialized or ethnic terms and to impute significant meaning to these differences. The reasons for this relate to the unique way in which the politics of exclusion operate for them. People of Asian ancestry in this country are relegated to the margins based on race and on what I call an *assumption of foreignness*. That is, they continue to be seen as somehow more Asian (or Chinese or Japanese) than American. Put another way, if white ethnics represent the racially and culturally dominant center, Asian ethnics stand two steps outside that inner circle. As a result, the center has yet to see or accept Asian ethnics as "real" Americans. The irony, however, is that Asian ethnics are probably more similar to than different from white ethnics in terms of lifestyle preferences and general values.

As the title of this book suggests, Asian ethnics are often portrayed in extreme and simplified terms, either as perpetually foreign or as honorary members of an exclusive party hosted by whites. I chose this title to play on the ways in which Asians are commonly understood. As I hope to make clear, however, their experiences clearly defy such a simplistic dichotomy. Further, while I argue that outsiders indeed perceive Asian ethnics as foreigners, I am not suggesting that they have passively accepted this definition of themselves. On the contrary, I argue that Asian ethnics have and continue to struggle against the broad, stereotypical identities imposed upon them. Our respondents show resistance and agency even in the face of broader forces that continually constrain their identity options (Burawoy et al., 1991).

In Chapter 2, I provide a review of the literature on ethnic salience for later generation Americans, emphasizing the distinction between white ethnic and racialized ethnic experiences. I also review the arguments both for and against the applicability of assimilation theory predictions for Asian ethnics. Chapters 3 through 6 contain the substantive findings from our interviews. In Chapter 3, I explore our respondents' memories of growing up, and the role ethnicity played in their childhoods, while in Chapter 4, I compare the influences of neighborhood demographics in shaping their early relationships to ethnicity. Chapter 5 outlines the erosion of cultural traditions in their adult lives, and Chapter 6 addresses the ways ethnicity and, increasingly, race are salient features of their identity. Chapter 7 summarizes our major findings and discusses the implications of the study.

This study is hardly an exhaustive examination of Asian ethnics. Nevertheless, I believe it captures a particular aspect of the Asian ethnic experience—one situated in both class and social privilege. I do not claim to speak for all middle-class Asian ethnics or to uncover the experiences of Asian ethnics from other class strata. It is my hope, however, that this study might spur others to pay greater attention to later-generation Asians both empirically and theoretically; they may represent only a small fraction of the Asian-American population today, but this will not always be the case. Given the tremendous growth in Asian immigration over the past few decades, the seeds for future generations of Asian ethnics have been planted. Clues to what may be in store for them are to be found in the experiences of current multigeneration Asian-Americans.

Racialized Ethnics ◈ CHAPTER 2
Compared to
White Ethnics
Visiting the
Theoretical Debates

I n the previous chapter I referred to Asian ethnics as racialized ethnics—some clarification is needed here. My use of the term draws on the work of scholars who maintain that race and ethnicity are conceptually and experientially exclusive (Almaguer 1994; Blauner, 1972; Espiritu, 1992; Nishi, 1989; Omi & Winant, 1994; Takaki, 1987, 1989a; Warner & Srole, 1945; Waters, 1992, 1990). As Mittelberg and Waters (1992) state, "[R]ace has been used by theorists to refer to distinctions drawn from physical appearance. Ethnicity has been used to refer to distinctions based on national origin, language, religion, food—and other cultural markers" (p. 425). I believe this to be an important distinction to make when examining the situation of Asian ethnics who, on one hand, may prefer to *define themselves* in ethnic terms (e.g., as Chinese or Japanese) to honor their ancestral roots but, on the other hand, may find themselves *being defined* in generically racial terms as Asian-Americans.

While the situation may be changing, race has been an

unproblematic aspect of identity for white Americans.[1] Most whites do not consciously consider how their racial status informs the world they see and experience. As the racial norm, the standard by which other groups are judged and deemed to deviate from, they have the social, political, and economic privilege to ignore their racialization (McIntosh, 1997). Accurately or not, many see themselves as *colorless* or racially neutral (Alba, 1990; Frankenberg, 1993; Lorde, 1984; Waters, 1990). Within the arena of ethnicity many white Americans have claimed a distinct group identity for themselves, *but only if they have chosen to do so.* This is what Waters (1986, 1990, 1992) means when arguing that white Americans have ethnic options to choose from—not only can they choose whether to assert an ethnic identity, they have the option of how much and which aspects of their ethnicity to incorporate into their lives.

A more problematic picture emerges for racial minorities who by definition are not part of the racial norm and whose identities are therefore consciously *racialized*, defined by and infused with racial meaning (Omi & Winant, 1994). Racial minorities can further be divided into racialized ethnic and strictly racial groups, the difference being that for the latter group, racial dimension is the salient marker, whereas for first group, ethnicity can also be a prominent feature of their identity. Racial minority groups, however, generally know that race shapes their perspectives on life, and they are aware of how race informs their experiences with others. The array of psychological, social, and structural privileges accompanying what Frankenberg (1993), Roediger (1991), and others (Haney-Lopez, 1996; McIntosh, 1997) refer to as "whiteness" does not benefit them.

For racialized ethnics, their racial and ethnic identities cross-cut and compete with each other for dominance, with race almost always overriding ethnicity. Mittelberg and Waters's (1992) work on middle-class Haitian immigrants is an excellent example. The pair effectively show how socially assigned and structurally imposed racial identities as blacks in the United States overshadow their respondents' self-defined ethnic identities as Haitians. Their respondents expressed frustration and ambivalence toward the post-immigration identity assigned to them that does not agree with their own Caribbean conceptions of race and blackness, which rely on a more nuanced combination of class and skin color criteria. Arguably, this racial-ethnic identity dilemma should be more pronounced for racial groups not composed of immigrants since the expectation of having identity options as the birthright of longtime Americans directly clashes with larger social practices of racial categorization, lumping, and homogenization (Espiritu, 1992, 1994; Nagel, 1994; Omi & Winant, 1994; Stanfield, 1993). For example, while a woman may wish to be identified as a fourth-generation Japanese-American, she may encounter stubborn resistance to being recognized along such nuanced lines and instead be seen only as an Asian-American or "Oriental" by whites who, by occupying the racial and cultural center, hold the power to define her. Alternatively, she may not wish to identify along racial or ethnic lines at all but finds people insisting on identifying her in this manner. The term *racialized ethnic* acknowledges the problematic nature of ethnicity for individuals who reside in the racial margins by: (1) recognizing the extension of racial meaning to ethnicity, a concept intended to signify cultural distinctions; and (2) considering the personal, social, and political struggle that often takes place between their self-defined identity (ethnic or otherwise) and socially imposed racial identity (Espiritu, 1992; Jiobu, 1988; Nagel, 1994; Phinney, 1990).

The Assimilation Paradigm—Its Supporters and Critics

The notion of a racialized ethnic experience distinct from a white ethnic experience is not universally agreed upon in the research literature. This discord is rooted in the larger theoretical debate over the applicability of the traditional assimilation model, as based on the white ethnic experience, for understanding the histories of racial minority groups in this country (Blauner 1972; Chan, 1991b; Espiritu, 1992, 1994; Stanfield, 1993; Takaki, 1987, 1989b).

Supporters of the paradigm argue that differences between white and racial minority experiences are ones of degree rather than kind (Kristol, 1972; Sowell, 1981). All groups undergo a period of struggle and adversity, even outright rejection, before they are allowed to join the ranks of the mainstream (Warner & Srole 1945). Irish and Italian immigrants, for example, experienced intense discrimination and "racial" prejudice as they struggled toward respectability (Alba, 1985a, 1985b; Roediger, 1991). With the passage of time, however, sociocultural, economic, and political differences have diminished for these groups as have specific ethnic allegiances. Arguably, these same processes are currently under way for black Americans, Asian-Americans, and other racialized groups although perhaps at a slower pace because of differences in social, political, and cultural contexts.[2] Or, perhaps variance in assimilation rates may relate to a misfit between the cultural values of some racial minority groups and what has come to be called the Protestant ethic values of the white American mainstream (Sowell, 1981). The point to emphasize here is that assimilation is seen as a linear and racially blind process whereby, as each generation becomes further removed from the original immigrants, the salience of ethnicity and its meaning in their lives weakens (Gordon, 1964; Park, 1950; Warner & Srole, 1945). These predictions and the model that they are based on are derived from the experiences of white ethnics, the descendants of earlier European immigrants.

▨ The White Ethnic Experience

> As you develop your own family celebrations, remember: It doesn't really matter how the traditions come to be or even what they are—you can continue customs from your childhood, combine aspects of your different heritages, or even borrow a great idea from a book or TV show. The only real goal is to create events your family can call its own. (Spencer, 1996, p. 167)

Welcome to the world of American family traditions, 1990s style. In this world parents are unapologetic about their sources for cultural inspiration. Each family unit picks and chooses what to cherish and uphold—the sky is the limit. This is a world where the motto is "if it feels good, go ahead and incorporate it as your own." Their children, in turn, will someday have the same discretion to continue the traditions they were raised with, modify them, or discard them altogether and start anew.

This passage, taken from a popular magazine dedicated to contemporary parenting, is revealing for what it discloses about ethnic observance and family traditions in a postmodern America—notice how the author simply assumes that parents in a typical American (read: white) family have different ethnic heritages. The assumption is correct; not only are endogamous marriages the exception today, most white parents are themselves the products of interethnic marriages and can claim two or more ethnic identities (Alba, 1990, 1995; Alba & Chamlin, 1983; Gans, 1979; Lieberson & Waters, 1988). Furthermore, most white ethnics have no direct ties to their country of origin, no kin or elders with ethnic memories to share, and subsequently no ongoing opportunities for exposure to ethnic languages, customs, or values (Alba, 1990, 1995; Crispino, 1980; Kellogg, 1990; Lieberson & Waters, 1988; Steinberg, 1989; Waters, 1990, 1992). Suburbanization has further eroded the overlapping network of primary and secondary ethnic relationships that in the past functioned to maintain a cohesive ethnic community (Cohen, 1977; Yancey, Ericksen, & Juliani, 1976). Today, one hardly knows or cares about the ethnicity of one's neighbors (although the same cannot be said for racial differences) (Waters, 1990).

Clearly, the ethnic boundaries that mattered most in the past have undergone a fundamental transformation (Alba, 1990). The average white American no longer thinks of him or herself primarily in ethnic terms. Ethnicity typically trails behind professional, familial, or social roles. To identify ethnically, to make it a prominent feature of one's identity, requires a conscious choice (Alba, 1990; Waters, 1990).

That contemporary white ethnics have been cast ethnically adrift by these changes in social structure and interrelationships has proved fertile ground for sociologists interested in processes of ethnic construction and transmission. What role, for instance, can ethnicity play in families where such heterogeneity exists? Do parents expose their children to all their ethnic heritages, some, or none? Furthermore, which aspects of those heritages do they emphasize or incorporate into their family's lives, if any at all?

Current empirical research offers some thought-provoking answers to these questions and others about contemporary white
ethnicity. Both Alba (1990) and Waters (1990) find, for instance,
that ethnicity plays only a marginal role in the family life of white
ethnics. Parents are not particularly concerned with transmitting
ethnic knowledge to their children nor do they go to much effort
in exposing their children to their cultural heritages.

> Only a minority of parents want their children to identify, and
> an even smaller minority take forthright steps to encourage
> them to do so. If the identities of the next generation depend
> on the decisions and actions of contemporary parents, then
> ethnic identity will undergo a decline in the future, for par-
> ents are more likely to identify themselves than to want their
> children to do so. (Alba, 1990, p. 205)

Furthermore, there is a tendency toward ethnic simplification—
picking, choosing, and identifying with only parts of their authentic ancestry. An example is identifying only with the father's
ancestry rather than the exact combination of both parents' ancestries. Or, more capricious factors such as appearance ("I look
more Irish than I do German"), surname, or the relative popularity of different ethnic ancestries may be the basis for the choice
(Waters, 1990). There is also a growing trend toward identifying
panethnically as a Euro-American, thereby acknowledging and pay-
ing tribute to a general descendance from any European country
(Alba, 1990).

When they do choose to assert their ethnic identity, white
ethnics generally do so in ways that have little bearing on their
daily lives: "It does not, for the most part, limit choice of marriage
partner (except in almost all cases to exclude nonwhite ethnics).
It does not determine where you will live, who your friends will
be, what job you will have, or whether you will be subject to discrimination" (Waters, 1990, p. 147). Instead, ethnicity centers
largely around the warm, nostalgic, and generally positive *feelings*
they associate with being a member of an ethnic community
(Bershtel & Graubard, 1992; Kellogg, 1990; Zenner, 1985). Claim-

ing an ethnic identity allows whites to feel unique in a social milieu that currently celebrates and commercializes ethnic foods, festivals, music, and clothing. In short, ethnicity has taken on a largely superficial function and is now a "leisure-time activity" to be taken up in one's free time (Gans, 1979).

Alba (1990) attributes four essential features to this "new" form of ethnicity exhibited by white ethnics. First, salience and intensity vary widely because it is dependent upon the personal inclinations and proclivities of individuals. Second, the few and intermittent ethnic experiences they engage in are largely shallow in content. Third, ethnicity is often confounded with family history that, Alba argues, "amounts to a privatization of ethnic identity— a reduction of its expression to largely personal and family terms" (p. 300). Fourth, ethnicity is no longer tied into active social structures or communal interaction. Most white ethnics see no disjuncture between claiming a salient ethnic identity and yet engaging in almost no interaction with coethnics.

None of this is to suggest that white Americans no longer identify ethnically; on the contrary, many continue to do so, albeit generally in hyphenated terms as Irish-Americans, Italian-Americans, and the like (Alba, 1990; Lieberson & Waters, 1988). And there are, of course, individuals as well as religiocultural groups such as the Amish for whom ethnicity remains a significant part of their identity and lives, thus influencing their choice of spouse, friends, neighbors, and attitudes toward social issues (Greeley, 1971, 1974; Novak, 1973). Clearly, the meanings the majority of white Americans today attach to their ethnic identities have changed (Waters 1990). As Gans (1979) argues, ethnicity is increasingly a "leisure-time" or "symbolic" activity acknowledged only intermittently, for instance, during the holidays or the occasional ethnic festival. Whether identifying ethnically carries any significant meaning for them or influences how they conduct their daily lives is questionable. Plainly, whether to identify ethnically, which parts to identify with, and what actions to be taken to demonstrate one's ethnic loyalties has become a personal choice. Ethnicity, as Waters (1990) argues, "is not something that influences their lives unless they *want* it to" (p. 7).

The Racialized Ethnic Experience

Whether ethnicity has declined to the same extent or in the same ways for the descendants of non-European groups is much less clear. Much of the ethnic identity literature, based largely on the European-American experience, has remained silent regarding its applicability to racial minorities who have resided in the United States for multiple generations.[3] This silence reflects the belief that the white ethnic experience is not fundamentally different from the racialized ethnic experience (Chavez, 1991; Kristol, 1972; Park, 1950; Petersen, 1972; Sowell, 1981).

An extensive counter-assimilationist literature has emerged, however, vehemently arguing that the experiences of African-Americans, Asian-Americans, and other racial minority groups differ markedly from Americans of European origin (Almaguer, 1994; Barrerra, 1979; Blauner, 1972; Chan, 1991b; Lieberson, 1981; Lieberson & Waters, 1988; Omi & Winant, 1994; Takaki, 1987, 1989a, 1989b). Owing to the significance of socially defined racial categories and the status and material inequities they produce, racial minorities do not have the option to follow the assimilation path that their white counterparts have taken. While racial minority groups, in particular members of the middle class, have acculturated, that is, adopted the broader values and culture of the white mainstream, the same level of social, political, and economic acceptance afforded white ethnics has not characterized their assimilation experience (Almaguer, 1994; Blauner, 1972; LaFromboise, Coleman, & Gerton, 1993; Matusow, 1989; Omi & Winant, 1994; Takaki, 1989b; Walton, 1989; Warner & Srole, 1945). Instead, as Broom and Kitsuse (1955) argued more than forty years ago, racial minorities are still marginalized because their assimilation has lacked validation by the dominant white mainstream that continues to classify and treat them as "other." Whether or not members of racial groups are practicing ethnics in the traditional sense (speak the language of the ancestral homeland, prepare ethnic foods, participate in ethnic organizations, etc.), an ethnic identity is imposed on them by virtue of their physical appearance, and ultimately they are seen as less authentically American than their white ethnic counterparts.

Discussions of symbolic ethnicity seldom mention blacks, Mexicans, Asians, Native Americans, or other nonwhite groups. Because of physiological distinctiveness, they cannot become an invisible part of the white mass, and so they cannot volunteer away their ethnicity as easily as many European groups. (Jiobu, 1988, p. 12)

The question why racial distinctions should so profoundly structure and shape social life naturally arises. While the decisive answer to this vexing question remains to be found, sociologists of the American racial landscape have leaned toward historical explanations that examine initial contact between European settlers and non-European groups and the racial ideologies that developed as the settlers and their descendants colonized and dominated this country (Almaguer, 1994; Blauner, 1972; Blumer, 1958; Horsman, 1981; Omi & Winant, 1994; Steinberg, 1989). Through conquest, genocide, slavery, and exclusion, Americans of European ancestry effectively established a rigid racial hierarchy, placing themselves at the top. The very definition of what it has meant to be an American has demanded descendancy from European (better yet, Anglo-Saxon and Protestant) stock (Glazer, 1993; Higham, 1963).

As times have changed, however, this image of a white America has been sorely challenged. Since the Civil Rights Movement, racial groups have increasingly demanded recognition of their place in American history and their contributions to building this country (Blauner, 1972; Omi & Winant, 1994; Takaki, 1993). These protests have forced dialogues regarding America's multiracial and multicultural past and present. Nevertheless, efforts to rewrite American history have met fierce opposition. As Alba (1990) argues, what it means to be an American continues to imply ancestry from any part of Europe. Whites continue to feel a sense of "proprietary claim," to use Herbert Blumer's (1958) classic terminology, to being the "real" Americans. As racial minority groups continue to make demands for inclusion in this title, some whites have become increasingly defensive and resentful toward what they feel is an encroachment upon their unique claim to being American. This reluctance to expand the boundaries of "Americanness" to include racial minorities, critics contend, continues to thwart their efforts to gain full social, political, and economic acceptance.

▨ *The Asian Ethnic Case*

The situation of Asian-Americans in general and of Asian ethnics in particular, takes on special significance in light of the previous discussion since their experiences have been taken to support as well as critique the assimilation paradigm. A review of both arguments, which I refer to as the "honorary white" versus "forever foreign" positions, follows.

Asian Ethnics as "Honorary Whites"

Supporters of the single path model of assimilation frequently cite the achievements of Asian-Americans to bolster their position that all groups regardless of race can succeed (Glazer & Moynihan, 1975; Petersen, 1966, 1972; Sowell, 1981; Tinker, 1982). Despite an earlier history of intense racial prejudice, Asian-Americans have come far in gaining social acceptance and economic stability—achievements seemingly impossible to attain if race alone were an impassable barrier to mobility (Fugita & O'Brien, 1991b; Hirschman, 1983; Hirschman & Wong, 1981; Jiobu, 1988; Montero, 1980; Nee & Sanders, 1985; Nee & Wong, 1985; Rose, 1985). Today, they are considered "model minorities," upstanding and high achieving individuals reputed for their work ethic and perseverance (Bell, 1985; Divorky, 1988; McBee, 1984; Min, 1995; Osajima, 1988; Sue & Okazaki, 1990). Newspaper headlines such as, "Why Do Asian Pupils Win Those Prizes?";[4] "Why Asians Succeed Here";[5] and "Asian-Americans: A Model Minority";[6] are typical of the stories that surface each year extolling this group's achievements, particularly in the area of higher education. Statistics showing the Asian-American presence at major universities to be well in excess of their percentage in the general population fuel such captions.

Thanks in part to such profuse publicity, scholars and lay persons alike tout Asian-Americans as the newest additions to the American mainstream, the most recent in a long procession of ethnic groups to have climbed up the social hierarchy and "arrived."

Table 2.1   ▒   *Education by Nativity (18 years and over)*
State of California

	Native-Born Chinese	Native-Born Japanese	Native-Born Whites*
12th Grade, No Diploma	6.84	7.41	15.10
High School Graduate	14.43	22.43	25.02
Some College	33.47	34.00	35.48
College Graduate	30.88	26.28	16.26
Post B.A. Degree	14.38	9.88	8.15
Total	100	100	100
N	(96,429)	(167,354)	(13,300,0000)

SOURCE: 1990 U.S. Census PUMS 5% for the state of California.
*Non-Hispanic Whites.

Some even argue that they may be undergoing "whitening"[7] processes similar to those experienced by southern, central, and eastern European immigrants earlier in the century (Alba, 1985b, 1990; Glazer, 1993; Hacker, 1992; Loewen, 1971; Lyman, 1986; Montero, 1980; Tinker, 1982; Warren & Twine, 1994). These sentiments, in turn, have earned Asian-Americans the curious designation of "honorary whites." Demographic data that paint an optimistic picture of their economic and social standing largely inform such opinions.

Census Data for the State of California[8]

On the surface the chances for a successful material life for native-born Chinese- and Japanese-Americans do not differ markedly from native-born whites. In fact, both Asian ancestry groups surpass native-born whites on a number of key social and economic indicators. As Table 2.1 illustrates, a significantly higher percentage of both Asian ancestry groups have earned a college degree (30.88 percent and 26.28 percent, respectively) compared to their white counterparts (16.26 percent). A higher percentage of both groups have also earned post-B.A. degrees (14.38 percent and 9.88 percent, respectively) compared to whites (8.15 percent), although the difference between Japanese and whites is small.

These figures are not particularly surprising in light of media

Table 2.2 ▨ *Occupational Status for Native-Born,*
State of California

	Native-Born Chinese	Native-Born Japanese	Native-Born White*
Executive, Administrator, Manager	16.85	15.96	15.02
Professional Specialty	23.51	21.63	16.09
Technician	6.87	5.63	3.76
Sales	12.83	11.68	13.63
Administrative Support	21.09	19.94	17.50
Service	7.17	6.64	11.05
Farming, Forestry, Fishing	0.70	4.66	1.70
Precision, Craft, Repair	5.27	6.62	10.78
Machine, Assembler, Inspector	2.02	3.09	3.27
Transportation, Moving	3.68	4.06	6.74
Military	0.01	0.09	0.45
Total	100	100	99.99**
N	(87,473)	(146,228)	(10,980,000)

SOURCE: 1990 U.S. Census PUMS 5% for the state of California.
*Non-Hispanic Whites.
**Totals do not add up to 100% due to rounding error.

accounts of Asian-Americans' educational achievements and seemingly sudden explosion into higher education. Take what has happened at the University of California at Berkeley (U.C.B.) as an example. As recently as 1966, Asian-American students accounted for less than one in twenty undergraduates;[9] in 1995 they accounted for roughly seven out of every twenty undergraduates, phenomenal growth within a period of thirty years (Institute for the Study of Social Change, 1991; Takagi, 1992). At the University of California at Irvine (U.C.I.), the figures are even more remarkable; in the 1996–97 academic year, Asian-Americans made up approximately half of the entire student population. The same statistics hold at the other campuses—Asian-Americans have emerged as a major force in the University of California (U.C.) system, which is amazing when one considers that they compose only a little more than 9 percent of the state's population (U.S. Census, 1993b).

Education is not an end in itself, however. Many native-born Chinese- and Japanese-Americans have successfully cashed in their

Table 2.3   ▧ Family Income by Nativity,
                 State of California

	Native-Born Chinese	Native-Born Japanese	Native-Born White*
Less than 9,999	7.84	6.05	10.41
10,000–19,999	7.37	6.83	11.81
20,000–29,999	8.94	10.21	13.26
30,000–39,999	11.32	11.01	13.63
40,000–49,999	11.92	12.32	12.19
50,000+	52.61	53.58	38.70
Total	100	100	100
N	(207,409)	(212,174)	(17,720,163)

SOURCE: 1990 U.S. Census PUMS 5% for the state of California.
*Non-Hispanic Whites.

degrees for white-collar jobs (see Table 2.2). Particularly noteworthy is the category, Professional Specialty, comprising a wide array of professions demanding high skills and educational training. Both native-born Chinese and Japanese have the greatest proportion of workers in this category.

Native-born Chinese and Japanese were also more likely to report family incomes that equaled or exceeded $50,000 compared to white ethnics (see Table 2.3). A little more than half of native-born Chinese and Japanese families earned $50,000 or more (52.61 percent and 53.58 percent, respectively) compared to a little more than a third of white families (38.70 percent).

Statistical data showing low rates of residential segregation (compared with blacks and Hispanics) and rising intermarriage rates are further indicators that the social boundaries that separated Asian-Americans from the larger society are dissolving (Barringer, Gardner, & Levin, 1993; Kitano, Yeung, Chai, & Hatanaka, 1984; Lee & Yamanaka, 1990; Massey & Denton, 1987; Min, 1995; Montero, 1980; Sung, 1990; Tinker, 1982; Warren & Twine, 1994; White, Biddlecom, & Guo, 1993; Wong, 1989). According to Min (1995), Asian-Americans nationwide are overrepresented in suburban residential areas. Each major Asian group (Chinese, Japanese, Korean, Filipino, Indian, Vietnamese) has a higher level of residence in urban fringes, suburban areas lying just

Table 2.4 ☒ *Intermarriage Rates by Sex for Native-Born, State of California*

	Chinese		Japanese	
	Male	Female	Male	Female
Same Ethnicity	57.10	51.70	60.50	50.40
Intermarried	42.90	48.30	39.50	49.60
Total	100	100	100	100
N	(32,881)	(33,425)	(61,700)	(66,879)

SOURCE: Modified from Shinagawa and Pang (1996).

outside central cities than do whites, blacks, or Hispanics, a finding that suggests that Asian-Americans are successfully asserting their middle-class privilege to reside in desirable residential areas.

In addition, intermarriage rates are also on the rise as more native-born Asian-Americans are interacting both in and out of the workplace with individuals outside their ethnic group. According to Shinagawa and Pang's (1996) calculations, based on 1990 Census data for the state of California, 42.9 percent of all native-born and married Chinese men have outmarried compared to 39.5 percent of all native-born and married Japanese men (see Table 2.4). Corresponding figures for native-born and married Chinese and Japanese women are 48.3 percent and 49.6 percent, respectively.

These figures reflect a significant increase in both absolute number and proportion of all marriages since the 1980 Census. That nearly half of all native-born and married Chinese- and Japanese-American women have outmarried is dramatic and lends the strongest support for assimilation proponents who argue that intermarriage is a sign of social acceptance. These figures are in keeping with previous research indicating that Asian-American women are more likely to outmarry than Asian-American men (Fong & Yung, 1995; Kitano et al., 1984; Spickard, 1989; Sung, 1990; Weiss, 1973). While corresponding figures for native-born and married Chinese- and Japanese-American men are lower, they are remarkable nonetheless; roughly two out of every five have chosen to outmarry.

That so many native-born Chinese- and Japanese-Americans are outmarrying needs to be considered very carefully because of its implications, both practical and theoretical, for ethnicity's long-term salience. As Gordon (1964) argues, for intermarriages to occur in great numbers requires a significant breakdown of social barriers between the participating groups. Because of the extent to which Chinese and Japanese men and women in California are marrying, to concede that such barriers are becoming more permeable is not difficult. Nevertheless, caution should be used not to oversimplify this trend. To assume that the larger society will automatically embrace the children of such unions as one of "us," is problematic in light of this country's checkered history with mixed-race people (remember the one-drop rule?), the majority of whom have been treated largely as outcasts (King, 1997; King & DaCosta, 1996; Root, 1992; Zack, 1992, 1995, 1996). As the recent mixed-race movement attests, quite possibly rather than assimilating into the white majority, biracial and multiracial people may form a distinct racial category.[10]

What is also not clear from these figures are the changes that have been taking place in terms of whom Asian ethnics marry when they intermarry. Typically, the most attention has been paid to intermarriages between whites and Asians. According to Shinagawa and Pang (1996), however, interethnic marriages at the aggregate level have surpassed interracial marriages with whites in the last ten years. That is, marriages between different Asian ethnic groups (Chinese-Japanese, Korean-Chinese, Filipino-Japanese, etc.) now outnumber marriages between whites and native-born Asians. For native-born and intermarried Chinese- and Japanese-Americans, interethnic marriages exceeded interracial marriages with whites for all subgroups except Japanese-American women, although the difference is less than 1 percent (see Table 2.5).

These are powerful findings. Without question, group boundaries are changing, but what appears to be happening are parallel processes of dissolving boundaries. On one side are those who are merging with members of the racial majority (white Americans) and are therefore following the predicted pattern for marital assimilation. On the other side are those who are choosing partners who share a common panethnic or racialized identity as Asian-Americans (Chan & Hune, 1995; Espiritu, 1992; Min, 1995; Omi, 1993; Shinagawa & Pang, 1996; Wei, 1993). While these marriages

Table 2.5   Intermarriage Rates by Sex and Race for Native-Born, State of California

| | Chinese | | Japanese | |
	Male	Female	Male	Female
Same Ethnicity				
Spouse	57.10	51.70	60.50	50.40
Asian Spouse	23.90	24.40	20.60	22.40
White Spouse	15.40	20.90	14.60	23.10
NonAsian/				
Nonwhite Spouse	3.60	3.00	4.20	4.20
Total	100	100	100	100
N	(32,881)	(33,425)	(61,700)	(66,879)

SOURCE: Modified from Shinagawa and Pang (1996).

are dissolving previously salient boundaries, the boundaries that are increasingly dissolving, then, are ethnic ones.

One has to wonder why since the last census, when the number of panethnic unions has surged, there has not been more made of this trend,[11] especially its potential effect on race relations. Shinagawa and Pang (1996) suggest that the trend ties in with a growing racial consciousness in American society:

> Deindustrialization, white flight, increased economic competition, anti-immigrant sentiments, hate violence against Asians, the growing sense of despair and hopelessness in the inner cities, and interracial conflicts not only between Whites and Asian Americans but also between racial minority groups all signify the importance of race in American society and have heightened the racial consciousness of Asian Americans. Race, increasingly more so than ethnicity, shapes the experiences and the development of identity among Asian Americans. (p. 144)

A growing racial consciousness, of course, runs counter to the predictions of assimilation theorists and is a particularly curious trend found among their best test case, those who have been dubbed "honorary whites." Why should native-born Asian-Americans develop a strong racial consciousness if, indeed, the situation is as rosy as portrayed by the media? Clearly, a closer look is needed to make sense of this finding.

Asian Ethnics as "Forever Foreign"

Critics of the assimilation paradigm and its relevance to Asian-Americans do not deny that Asian ethnics have made significant gains in the United States. What they dispute are the magnitude of those gains and their lack of uniformity across Asian ethnic groups, what the gains say about the level of social acceptance they have achieved, and how the model minority image pits Asian-Americans against other racial groups (Chan, 1991b; Huhr & Kim, 1989; Lee, 1996; S. M. Lee, 1989; Min, 1995; Nishi, 1989; Okihiro, 1994; Osajima, 1988; Suzuki, 1989). As Takagi (1992) argues:

> The concept of the model minority was born in the midst of the tumultuous racial change of the 1960s. Against the back-drop of rioting in black ghettos, the "long hot summers" of the late 1960s, and mass public demonstrations for civil rights, Asian-Americans appeared to be a relatively quiescent minority. . . . To many whites, Asian-American achievement sounded an encouraging note in what was otherwise a threatening and uncertain period of racial politics. Angered by black criticism of the "white establishment," some whites pointed to Asian-American achievement as evidence that racial minorities could get ahead in America, if only they would "try." (pp. 58–59)

The central complaint, however, is that Asian-Americans are still treated as illegitimate Americans and that rosy details of survey and census data do not convey this aspect of their experience (Chin, 1994; Fong, 1982; Lee, 1989; National Asian Pacific American Legal Consortium [NAPALC], 1997; Nishi, 1989; Takaki, 1989a; Wong, 1995; Yun, 1989). To support this claim, reference is commonly made to three key differences distinguishing the European from the Asian ethnic experience: generational and ethnic differences are ignored; rising anti-Asian sentiment; and questionable economic parity. Each factor, in turn, has implications for prolonging ethnic salience as well as the development of a racialized identity for Asian ethnics.

Table 2.6   Percentage Foreign-Born and Native-Born
             for Selected Asian-American Groups in
             the United States

	Foreign-Born	Native-Born
Asian (composite)	66	34
Chinese*	69	31
Filipino	64	36
Japanese	32	68
Asian Indian	75	25
Korean	73	27
Vietnamese	80	20

SOURCE: U.S. Bureau of the Census (1993).
*Excludes Taiwanese.

"American Beats Kwan": Generational and Ethnic Differences Are Ignored. Throughout their histories in this country, Asian-Americans and the communities they have formed have been subject to the whims of white policymakers (Hing, 1993). Various exclusionary laws enacted in the late nineteenth and early twentieth centuries, for example, were responsible for the virtual cessation of Asian immigration until the 1960s. Population growth up to that time had been almost entirely dependent upon natural reproduction (Min, 1995; Takaki, 1989b).

With the repeal of the last of these policies in 1965, immigration from Asia quickly gained momentum, and the Pacific Rim became a leading source of legal immigrants to the United States (Barringer et al., 1993; Fawcett & Cariño, 1987). While unintended, the 1965 Immigration Act set into motion forces which have dramatically altered the face, content, and character of Asian America. Today, as Table 2.6 illustrates, the majority of Asian-Americans nationwide (66 percent) are foreign born. The category Asian-American, however, is a composite that lumps together ethnic groups separated by socioeconomic, historical, and generational differences (Espiritu, 1992; Min, 1995). Chinese and Japanese, for example, began immigrating to the United States more than 150 years ago and today have sizable multigeneration populations (Takaki, 1989b). The Vietnamese, in contrast, have only a burgeoning second generation because of their recent arrival (Gold & Kibria, 1993).

The influx of Asian newcomers has undoubtedly influenced public perceptions of Asian-Americans because most Americans, white and nonwhite, are unable or unwilling to recognize ethnic much less generational differences between and within Asian groups (Hayano, 1981; Kitano, 1992). For instance, for a fourth-generation Chinese-American to be mistaken for a Korean immigrant is common. During times of doubt, all persons perceived to have Asian features are assumed to be newcomers to this country (Espiritu, 1992; Min, 1995; Omi, 1993). Media coverage highlighting hardworking Asian immigrant families, desperate Asian refugees, and more recently, shadowy foreign campaign donors, along with film and screen representations of thickly accented and socially awkward Asian immigrants, plainly have done little to dispel the foreigner image (Fong, 1998; Hamamoto, 1994; Kim, 1986).

Nevertheless, to attribute the foreigner image solely to new immigrants would be a mistake—their arrival has merely reinforced the image. As Lowe (1996) argues:

> A national memory haunts the conception of the Asian-American, persisting beyond the repeal of actual laws prohibiting Asians from citizenship and sustained by the ways in Asia, in which the Asian is always seen as an immigrant, as the "foreigner-within," even when born in the United States and the descendant of generations born here before. (p. 6)

Even before significant Asian immigration, most Americans saw Asian ethnics as more foreign than native to this country.[12] They were unassimilable foreigners, forever distinct as captured by the Orientalist discourse (Said, 1979). The wartime internment of Japanese-Americans, two-thirds of whom were native-born, illustrates this: "No matter how American the Nisei looked, felt, and acted, they could not avoid the traumatic rejection of their American identity that came their way during World War II" (Spickard, 1989, p. 33).

The American-born Chinese, at least most of them, are legally and qualitatively American citizens. But on account of the

physical earmarks of their ancestry, the average American re-
acts to them in the same way as their parents and classifies
them with the foreign-born Chinese. This makes the problems
of the American-born Chinese unique, different from that of
American-born Europeans. (Louis, 1931, p. 5)

This assessment, written more than sixty-five years ago, arguably
still holds true for Asian ethnics (Espiritu, 1992; Nishi, 1989;
Takaki, 1987, 1989a, 1989b; Wei, 1993). No matter how "Americanized," they are "still made conscious of their racial and ethnic
heritage by the larger society" (Wong, 1982, p. 79).

A recent gaffe on the part of MSNBC, the Internet news ven-
ture between Microsoft and NBC, captures this sentiment perfectly.
In announcing the gold medal winner of the 1998 Olympic Games
women's figure skating competition, MSNBC's headline boldly an-
nounced: "American beats Kwan." The skaters in question, Tara
Lipinski and Michelle Kwan, are, of course, both American. In the
full story, the article states: "American finishes strong to overtake
Kwan, who takes silver." While this unconscious slip surely speaks
poorly on behalf of the writer, it is also crucial to acknowledge the
larger social context in which such a gaffe could take place. Takaki's
(1989a) sentiments about the murder of Vincent Chin (to be discussed below), I believe, speak to this situation as well:

Our educational institutions have also contributed to this
tragic event: They have done so by omission. Their curricula,
from grade school to the universities, usually overlook or ignore the presence and contributions of Asian Americans.
"American" history and "American" literature courses leave
out knowledge about the immigrants who went east to America
and about their descendants. Consequently, they give the impression that "American" is "white." (p. 28)

Seen in this light the writer's gaffe makes all too much sense given
how Asian-Americans are portrayed (or not) in this country. Ultimately, being an American is equated with being white. And as a
result, Asian ethnics, despite being longtime Americans, lack the
option to cast aside their racial and ethnic affinities as European
ethnics, who by birthright are part of the American mainstream,

freely do (Maykovitch, 1972; Nishi, 1989; Takaki, 1987; Wei, 1993). Instead, the range of available identification labels is narrowly circumscribed or even imposed (Espiritu, 1992; Nagel, 1994; Uba, 1994; Yasutake, 1977). While choosing to identify as an Asian-American or a Chinese-American, Japanese-American, and so forth, may be legitimately recognized, choosing to self-identify as an unhyphenated American may not (Chin, 1994; Fong, 1982; Wei, 1993).

"Forget Pearl Harbor—Remember Detroit": Rising Anti-Asian Sentiment. One of the primary tenets of classic assimilation theory posits that social acceptance accompanies economic mobility (Gordon, 1964). In the case of Asian-Americans, material success has actually hastened greater resentment. From African-American communities feeling encroached upon by Korean merchants, to Detroit auto workers feeling threatened by Japanese automakers, to high school students feeling that Asian-American "curve busters" are filling all the available slots in higher education institutions,[13] Asian-Americans across the country have increasingly become the scapegoats for a range of economic and social ills. Shifting international relations with the Pacific Rim along with renewed Asian immigration have further contributed to a growing perception among Americans from various walks of life of an imminent "Asian invasion" (see Figure 2.1).

The campaign finance scandal involving foreign Asian donors and their attempts to gain political favors is the latest confirmation of this "looming" Asian threat. Savvy politicians, feeding off the fear already present, are furthering their own careers by exposing how Asians have infiltrated the political system of the United States with illegal foreign money. Never mind that all Asian-Americans, irrespective of nativity, are being used as collective scapegoats in the process or that other foreign investors have been found guilty of funneling money illegally or that the money in question amounts to less than 2 percent of total contributions made during the period in question (Guillermo, 1997). Frank Wu, a law professor at Howard University, put it best: "Nobody is defending wrongdoing. But if one person does something wrong, that doesn't mean that other people with similar names or faces or ancestry have done anything wrong."[14]

FIGURE 2.1. "Gook Invasion!" From NAPALC's *1996 audit of violence against Asian Pacific Americans.* Reproduced courtesy of the National Asian Pacific American Legal Consortium.

Not surprisingly, as perceptions of threat have grown so have incidences of anti-Asian hostility and hate crimes (Espiritu, 1992; Min, 1995; Nishi, 1989; Pimental, 1995; Takaki, 1989; U.S. Commission on Civil Rights, 1986, 1992). According to NAPALC (1997), violence directed against Asian Pacific Americans has steadily increased over the past four years, with a record 534 reported cases nationwide in 1996; this accounts for a 17 percent increase from the previous year when the FBI had reported that violent crimes were down 7 percent nationwide. Significantly, the perpetrators

of these crimes disregard differences between newly arrived immigrants and native-born Americans as well as ethnic differences
in choosing their victims (U.S. Commission on Civil Rights, 1986,
1992).

> The crimes, as reported to various Asian-American organiza-
> tions and to the police, range in violence from racist-graffiti
> on the offices of the Japanese-American Citizens League in
> Sacramento, to an attack on a Chinese-American family in [a]
> Vallejo, Calif., amusement park, where they were taunted and
> told to return to China, to the fire-bombing of the home of a
> Chinese city councilman in Sacramento. In a significant num-
> ber of incidents, attackers say, "Go home," or "Get out of my
> country," the [California State Attorney-General] report said.
> ("Attacks Against," p. A16)

As Espiritu (1992) argues: "In the Asian-American case, group
members can suffer sanctions for no behavior of their own, but
for the activities of others who resemble them" (p. 132). The killing of Vincent Chin, a 1.5 generation Chinese-American mistak-
enly accused of being a "job-stealing Jap," stands as the tragic
embodiment of this disregard for ethnic and generational differences (Nishi, 1989; Takaki, 1989a).

> On June 19, 1982, this twenty-seven-year-old Chinese-Ameri-
> can went to a Detroit bar with three friends to celebrate his
> upcoming wedding. There, two white auto workers—Ronald
> Ebens and his stepson, Michael Nitz—taunted him, reportedly
> calling him "Jap." Ebens complained: "It's because of you,
> motherfuckers, that we're out of work!" A brief scuffle ensued.
> Chin quickly left the bar, and was chased and hunted by Ebens
> and Nitz. They finally trapped Chin in front of a McDonald's
> restaurant where Nitz held their prey while Ebens bludgeoned
> him with a baseball bat. (Takaki, 1989a, p. 23)

Again, emphasis must be on the larger social climate in which this
killing took place—the economic slump Detroit's auto industry was
experiencing in the 1980s, the rise in popularity of Japanese cars,
and the sense of economic and social insecurity arising from these
conditions. Further, as Michael Moore (1988) writes, "Hate does

not well up spontaneously. It has historic roots, and it receives current encouragement from corporate executives, politicians, and media commentators" (p. 25) Moore offers proof to support this statement:

- Statements made by Chrysler Chairperson Lee Iacocca that flamed the sense of a foreign takeover: "The Japanese are coming in." "While we're trying to deal with things in the front yard, they're in the back yard taking over the country."
- Chrysler official Bennett Bidwell, former president of the Hertz Corporation, echoed his boss's feelings when he said the best way to deal with the trade imbalance would be to charter the *Enola Gay*, the B-29 that dropped the atomic bomb on Hiroshima.
- Popular bumper stickers bashing Japan: "Unemployment—Made in Japan"; "Honda, Toyota, Pearl Harbor"; "Forget Pearl Harbor—Remember Detroit"; "I'd rather eat worms than drive a Jap bike."
- News footage of unemployed auto workers taking a sledgehammer to a Japanese car.
- A CBS Evening News story that referred to Japanese imports as "the second Japanese invasion of the United States," complete with pictures of the bombing of Pearl Harbor to accompany the report.

So who killed Vincent Chin? This is the question filmmakers Christine Choy and Renee Tajima ask in their documentary of the same title. After reviewing the above remarks, the answer seems painfully clear; while Ebens may have dealt the death blow, many other faceless players were involved.

For critics of the "Asians as honorary whites" viewpoint, rising anti-Asian sentiment stands as a serious challenge to the notion that the American mainstream has genuinely accepted Asian-Americans as social equals. Rather, this hostility illustrates how their social acceptance is conditional and vulnerable to forces outside their control such as changing economic conditions or international relations (Omi, 1993). "Asian-Americans are keenly aware of changes in societal attitudes anytime there is news of trade conflict with an Asian country. Macrosocietal events are far beyond our control; yet they profoundly influence attitudes directed towards us" (Nishi, 1989, p. 4).

Questioned Economic Parity. Lastly, questions have been raised regarding the tendency of the media to overstate the economic progress of Asian-Americans and to ignore such issues as occupational glass ceilings and the great economic diversity that divides not only different Asian groups but native-born from foreign-born Asian-Americans (Barringer, Takeuchi, & Xenos, 1990; Chan, 1991b; Der, 1993; Hirschman & Wong, 1981; LEAP, 1993; Min, 1995; Wu, 1997). For example, the well-publicized incomes of Asian-American families have been contested on the grounds that they are actually the product of a greater number of workers per household compared with white households (Huhr & Kim, 1989; LEAP, 1994; Nee & Sanders, 1985; Uba, 1994). Moreover, Asian-Americans generally reside in states where wages (as well as the cost of living) tend to be higher, thus inflating nationwide figures for the general population: "Comparing the earnings of Asian-Americans who are concentrated in California to whites who more often reside in states where earnings are typically lower gives the false impression of higher earnings for Asian-Americans" (Nee & Sanders, 1985).

Then there are issues of underemployment and fair worth. The fruits of education are challenged. Because of blatant pay differentials and blocked mobility, Asian ethnics' extraordinary investment in education does not translate into incomes commensurate with similarly educated whites (Barringer et al., 1990; Chan, 1991b; Der, 1993; Hirschman & Wong, 1981; LEAP, 1994; Min, 1995). As Kent Wong, director of the U.C.L.A. Labor Center, remarks: "On the one hand, you have a higher number of professionals and college educated [Asian-American] employees than in the work force in general. However, you also have a situation where Asian-Americans have to have more education and training and years of experience in order to make salaries comparable to their white counterparts."[15] While they have achieved entry-level employment in a range of white-collar fields, glass ceilings supported by unflattering stereotypes block advancement into management ranks. As a recent *Asian Week* cover story put it, Asian-Americans suffer from the "worker bee syndrome"—good enough to be a grunt worker but not good enough to be a queen.[16]

Implications

Clearly, each of the factors discussed above has implications for racializing the identities of Asian ethnics or prolonging ethnic salience. Asian ethnics may feel compelled to identify ethnically even if it holds little meaning for them because others expect them to. As Kitano and Daniels (1988) assert, "[F]or Asian-Americans . . . the one inescapable fact is that of ethnic visibility, and reactions from the outside world force the retention of an ethnic identity, no matter how slight" (p. 191). Alternatively, Asian ethnics may embrace an ethnic or racial identity as a psychological lifeline in reaction to perceived hostility and rejection from the mainstream (Espiritu, 1992, 1994; Hosokawa, 1978; Kitano & Daniels, 1988; Maykovitch, 1972; Uba, 1994; Yasutake, 1977). Anti-Asian sentiment, in particular, has potential for heightening pan-Asian awareness, the recognition of common experiences and interests among various Asian subgroups (Espiritu, 1992; Omi, 1993). That all Asian-Americans are *potential victims* of racially motivated incidents can unite persons of Asian ancestry and thereby activate or enhance ethnic salience even if they have not personally suffered from a hate crime, racism, or prejudice in their own lives (Gordon, 1964). This, in fact, is exactly what happened in the wake of the Vincent Chin killing as scores of Asian-Americans across the nation rallied to protest the weak sentence imposed on Chin's killer (three years' probation and a fine of $3,780—neither man ever spent a day in jail).

Of course, quite possibly Asian ethnics retain salient ethnic identities for reasons that have little to do with those that critics of assimilation theory suggest, and these need to be taken into consideration. Rather than retaining salient ethnic identities in defensive reaction to social exclusion, Asian ethnics may be more inclined to maintain salient ethnic ties for reasons having nothing to do with external pressures. As Fugita and O'Brien (1991a) and Kendis (1989) argue, Japanese ethnics have been more successful in maintaining their ethnic identities simultaneous to assimilating at the structural level compared to their European ethnic counterparts. They attribute this ethnic propensity to traditional cultural factors "that structure social relationships among group members in such a way that they are able to adapt to changing exigencies without losing group cohesiveness" (Fugita & O'Brien, 1991a, p. 5).

Alternatively, Hansen's (1938) third-generation thesis suggests the possibility of later generation ethnics undergoing an ethnic revival. In other words, third-generation and later Asian ethnics may be "returning" to their ethnic roots now that they feel more secure of their place in America and have the economic resources to do so (Alba, 1990; Jiobu, 1988). Hansen developed his model, however, to explain a phenomenon observed to be taking place among European ethnics and did not take into consideration if and how racial differences might affect the perceived level of social security of an ethnic group. Further empirical work is needed to examine this issue.

Cars, Girls, and Baseball—but with an Asian Twist

CHAPTER 3

Growing Up Asian Ethnic

> We'd go to these little Japanese Obon festivals but those are just like, "Oh, let's eat some Japanese food and hang out with Japanese people once a year. And that was the extent of our Japanese heritage. My grandmother is more so but still it's kind of a novelty. (Ted Uyematsu)

We began our interviews by asking respondents to describe their families of origin, and the importance they placed on the transmission of ethnic traditions and values. We discovered parallels between their experiences growing up and those of white ethnics whom Waters (1990) and Alba (1990) had studied. Flexibility, fusion, and choice aptly characterize their early ethnic socialization. Similar to white ethnics, most respondents downplayed their parents' efforts to impart traditional cultural knowledge as well as the significance of what they were taught. We repeatedly heard comments similar to those made by Ron Kita,[1] a Sansei in his thirties,[2] who spoke with bemusement about his cultural indoctrination: "We never really got any Japanese culture you know.

48 ■

The only thing that I know is to take our shoes off before we enter the house, and we eat rice every night for dinner. That's about it."

Others spoke with equal candor about the seemingly superficial importance their parents placed on transmitting traditional cultural practices. While it would have been nice, most parents did not "go way out of their way" to ensure that their children were well versed. Rick Lew remarked: "They wanted their kids to have certain values that they considered Chinese, but it wasn't drastic." The prevailing attitude of their parents seems to have been one of casual interest in their children's ethnic socialization.

Because of the uniformity of their ethnic ancestry, it was surprising to learn of their parents' general disinterest in cultural transmittance. While extensive intermarriage complicates ethnic socialization for white ethnics, this is not so for most adult Asian ethnics today. All but three of our respondents are of homogenous ancestry.[3] That their parents did not place greater priority on cultural learning reveals much about the extent of acculturation that has taken place for them. After three generations or more in this society, they have not retained much of their cultural traditions despite possessing straightforward ancestries.

The transmission of cultural traditions was weak for both unintentional and intentional reasons. Unintentional reasons centered around their parents' own limited cultural knowledge combined with poor intergenerational communication. Intentional reasons included choosing not to carry on traditions viewed as outdated with their lifestyles and to avoid racial animosity.

"My parents don't have a whole lot to pass on": Unintentional Reasons

When asked about the importance her parents placed on retaining traditional Japanese culture, Karen Murakami, a fourth-generation Chinese-American (married to a Japanese-American), replied: "I think they tried. They wanted us to know something about their culture, as much as they knew. They didn't really grow up with a lot either." As second-, third-, and even fourth-generation Americans, most of their parents grew up more attuned to American mainstream culture than to traditional Chinese or Japanese culture.

Gary Hong, a law student in his twenties, shared his thoughts on his third-generation father:

> My dad is uniquely Chinese-American in the true sense. He's really Asian-American because he grew up in [pause] because his father passed away, he doesn't even speak Chinese. . . . I think there is a direct link there. So he does have a background in Chinese culture because he hung out with all these Chinese people in the Bay Area in that generation in Berkeley. There are a lot of Chinese people around, so he had the culture, he knows some of the stuff. He didn't practice it but he knew it. He hung around Chinese people a lot. He's definitely Chinese but a lot of the things they did as kids were like *Happy Days*, American stuff. Cars, girls, and baseball. That's kinda cool. So I look at all of them as Chinese-American.

Gary makes an important observation when stressing the cultural fusion that took place for his father's generation. Without denying the historical basis of culture, it is essential not to reify it either. Cultural values and practices are continually subject to reconstruction and redefinition (Nagel, 1994). Traditional Chinese culture was not simply transported across the ocean to the United States and then preserved in the same state as when the first Chinese came. A uniquely Chinese-American culture developed in this country, and within this cultural context, his father grew up. In turn, Gary's father adopted an ethnic identity fashioned from both Chinese and American elements. What his father passed on to Gary was not Chinese culture as traditionally defined, but what Yancey, Ericksen, and Juliani (1976) refer to as an emergent identity with practices centered around both Chinese and "American stuff," created and shared with coethnics and in some cases other Asian ethnics:

> My parents don't have a whole lot to pass on because my dad doesn't speak the language. The primary thing they could have passed on to me would be the language because both my grandparents and my parents don't do traditional stuff like lighting incense. We're all Christians so we don't do the Buddhist or Confucius things.
>
> *Q:* So what Chinese-American things did they pass on?

A: It's not really cultural, partly social. Being Chinese-American, being Asian-American, it's a combination of ideological, cultural, social. There is that social part because there is a community there. Just because they don't do traditional things like lighting incense in a temple doesn't mean that it's not a Chinese-American community. Chinese-American community in the sense that they do things together, they all understand each other, have a common background, look out for each other, do things in the community together. That's what they passed on to me. A recognition, they brought me up in that community, playing sports, doing things with their other friends. In that sense that's what they passed on to me. They passed on a Chinese-American culture to me, not as much a Chinese culture.

Gary's comments bring home the unfixed and fluid nature of culture and ethnicity (Nagel, 1991, 1994). Culture continually evolves and adjusts to the changing conditions in which it finds itself. It is also telling that Gary speaks of being Chinese-American and Asian-American interchangeably. As will be discussed in greater detail in Chapter 6, the criteria for community that Asian ethnics such as Gary are increasingly recognizing now include racial rather than strictly ethnic features.

Seen within this context, it is understandable why their parents did not place more emphasis on learning traditional culture. While certainly not against their children acquiring such knowledge, most parents simply did not go "way out of their way" to ensure they did. Exposing them to a range of cultural events and then giving them the choice to seek further knowledge was the favored approach. Kristi Kamamura's observation, "they didn't do it forcefully," aptly captures the sentiment of the majority of respondents on the topic of traditional cultural transmission.

Those who did not grow up in Asian-centered communities remembered being taken to ethnic museums, art exhibits, performances, and festivals. Such "ethnic snippets" were sporadic, however, and seldom made an enduring impression. Instead, activities usually added up to an erratic patchwork of cultural exposure with little lasting value. Respondents who grew up in Asian-centered communities, on the other hand, had a somewhat different experience since they did not need to rely on their families for cultural exposure. The nature of the communities they lived in provided them with more opportunities for cultural exposure. This topic is discussed further in Chapter 4.

"They'll buy a tray of moon cakes":
Honoring Ethnic Holidays

As for celebrating ethnic holidays, most did not recall great importance being placed on these events during their youth. As children, Chinese-Americans celebrated Chinese New Year's (the start of the new year as dictated by the lunar calendar) and the Moon Festival. Japanese-Americans celebrated the Obon festival, Boy's/Girl's Day, and New Year's (January 1). Most, however, downplayed the importance of these celebrations and were somewhat sarcastic about the ways their families celebrated. Rick Lew:

> They celebrate New Year's [pause], and I don't know if you can consider it celebrating, but during the Moon Festival, they'll buy a tray of moon cakes [laugh]. That's about the extent of our celebration of the Moon Festival.

As this excerpt illustrates, ethnic celebrations typically had an air of novelty to them. Families loosely celebrated these events rather than observing them with reverence.

There were some exceptions. Once again, respondents who grew up in Asian-centered communities recalled celebrating ethnic holidays with greater fanfare because of the excitement generated throughout the community. Older respondents, especially, described their memories of celebrations with rich texture and imagery. Peter Gong, a third-generation Chinese-American who grew up in San Francisco's Chinatown in the late 1920s, spoke of the *laycee* he received as a child during the Chinese New Year celebration. Laycee are red envelopes filled with money and customarily given to children during the New Year celebration.

> The only time we laid low was Chinese New Year's. Everybody would take off [from work] for a couple of weeks. We'd get dressed up, visit relatives and friends. The laycee. In those days

you didn't have packaged envelopes. They were all made by
hand. They were two and a half inches high, one and a half
deep. Red paper, eight and a half in square, folded. If we were
very good, we may get a quarter. But a dime was quite choice.
I don't remember getting a penny, but I wouldn't have thrown
it away. I used to pick up pennies. I still do. After you got the
laycee, you would have to clasp your hands together and pray
to the person in front of you. You do that quite seriously with
elder relatives.

Other exceptions include respondents whose family lineage in the
United States was less than straightforward. A handful of Japanese
ethnics had a *kibei* parent, the Japanese word for individuals born
in the U.S. but schooled abroad; one respondent had two kibei parents. Another handful consisted of individuals with one immigrant
parent. That at least one of their parents had a direct link to the
homeland and was thus more attuned to traditional Chinese or
Japanese culture distinguished these respondents. They grew up
in households where families observed traditional customs and
holidays with more reverence.

"Wiener teriyaki": Ethnic Foods

Eating ethnic foods was one of the few cultural practices most of
our respondents' parents observed regularly. The one food item
repeatedly mentioned by both Chinese and Japanese ethnics as a
dietary mainstay was rice. Even when families prepared non-
Chinese or non-Japanese food, rice was typically available as a side
dish: "We would have spaghetti too, but there would be rice there
too." Moreover, respondents made a point to emphasize that the
rice was not of the "Uncle Ben" variety but, rather, "authentic
stuff," long-grain or Japanese "sticky" rice.

While demanding authentic rice, main dishes were held to less
stringent criteria. Barry Sato,

It's hard to tell [how often we ate Japanese food] because most
things were a combination of a little bit of Japanese style cooking with western ingredients. We would always have the hamburger mixture, we have hamburger, the ground hamburger

with egg with onion and sugar and soy sauce. . . . We would have wiener teriyaki.

The humor of some food creations was not lost on our respondents. Many spoke sheepishly about their family's creative interpretations of traditional ethnic foods. Both Ted Uyematsu and Gary Hong were only mildly successful in veiling their sarcasm:

> [Ted] There's, uhm, kind of like a bastardization of Japanese food. Kind of like [pause] my grandmother would cook Japanese food, but it wasn't really authentic, and my family would cook even less authentic stuff. It was like, sure this is Japanese. They just attach some Japanese name to it, but it didn't resemble it at all.

> [Gary] See, it's hard to tell [how often we ate Chinese food] because, again, it would always be such a mix, you know. 'Cause like you have stir fry, is that Chinese? If you have stir fry and rice? 'Cause it's just vegetables and rice basically.

The creation of wiener teriyaki, odd as it may sound, provides another example of the continuing mixing of cultural elements that form an emergent culture. Our respondents lived in households where aspects of their ethnic culture, here in the area of food, merged with American culture. Combining Japanese sauce with a German sausage (a mainstay of American fare) is a telling symbol of the cultural blending that has taken and continues to take place.

"Everything's been diluted out": Other Ethnic Activities

Other adolescent memories included learning how to use chopsticks, memorizing ethnic words or phrases, and taking special classes (e.g., language school, karate/judo, Japanese dancing, playing the koto). It was the rare person, however, who participated in any activity on a long-term basis; most were discarded once they were not deemed "fun" or after family members stopped taking the initiative or planning events. As a child Susan Mineta, a Sansei in her fifties, was one of those exceptions:

Q: Did you practice any cultural traditions growing up?

A: Yes. For one thing the Japanese dancing during the Obon Festival. My mom made me take lessons for about four or five years to dance in the summertime. My grandmother bought me a kimono from Japan, and it's very special. In fact, I cherish those times much more now than I did then. I think it's important, you know, to have a little bit of background. That, and then New Year's was very traditional. A regular Japanese New Year. I liked the way we celebrated. We don't do it anymore these past years. And my mother and her sisters are getting old and don't feel like cooking all this stuff. And they don't get together, and I'm really sad because my husband's side of the family is very different than ours because they're from Hawaii, and their New Year's is not like ours. And I really miss it [pause] a lot.

I don't know if you know what *moochi* is. It's a rice cake that you make typically for New Year's, and you stack it with a tangerine on top and put it out for the living, for the dead, for pets, and put it up for good luck. It's just traditional to ring in the new year. My parents do it, and I do it because I want Danny [her son] to have something because he hardly has [pause] I mean, if you didn't look at him you wouldn't know he's Japanese. I mean he isn't very Japanese. One, even more than my friends I still eat with chopsticks. I don't like to eat with a fork because that's the way I grew up. But my son, he knows how to use them but not as much as I do. Everything's been diluted out, and I think that's really sad. I try to use the words I know for him so that he will use the Japanese word for rice, but he seems to have turned it around on me, and I now use "rice" instead of the Japanese word for it. That's kinda sad.

Susan was unique because she took traditional folk dancing lessons for a number of years instead of weeks. While acknowledging she may have had a different attitude back then, today warmth and nostalgia fill Susan's recollection of her childhood memories. Now a mother struggling to instill a sense of ethnic identity in her Yonsei son, she appreciates the need to have "a little bit of background." But Susan's tone in this passage reflects sad resignation. She laments the dilution taking place in her son's ethnic life, yet she has done little to stem the tide.

This passage points to the increasingly voluntary nature of

ritual observance for Asian ethnics and aptly illustrates the gradual weakening of ethnic salience within a family spanning three generations. Susan's Nisei mother and aunts no longer celebrate New Year's the way they did during her childhood because they "don't feel like cooking all this stuff, and they don't get together." Susan, in turn, has not accepted the responsibility of preparing the New Year's meal despite her fondness for this holiday. While she has carried on the tradition of setting out the rice cake display at New Year's so her son can get a taste of his Japanese heritage, she admits it has not had much influence. Susan has not successfully fostered a salient Japanese identity in her son who, in her own words, "isn't very Japanese." Despite being an exception in her own youth, she has raised a son who conforms to the general pattern we found in the majority of our respondents. This pattern suggests that what was once an unquestioned expectation—to observe ethnic holidays in ritual fashion—has become vulnerable to personal inclinations and superficial observance.

"My mom belongs to a Chinese bowling club": *Emergent Activities and Identities*

Where parents preferred to focus their energies was in encouraging their children to develop a healthy hyphenated Chinese-American or Japanese-American identity, associate with coethnics, and be part of a larger Asian-American or coethnic community of friends. In this respect, their parents differed from white ethnic parents; they placed greater emphasis on coethnic association and were more proactive persuading their children to interact with others like themselves. Respondents who did not grow up in Asian-centered communities, for example, remembered being encouraged to seek out coethnics or other Asian-American children in school. They also recalled their parents' placing them in situations where they would meet other Asian kids including ethnic churches (Christian and Buddhist), sports programs sponsored by ethnic organizations, Boy/Girl Scouts chapters consisting of coethnics, and language schools.

Karen Flores provides an example. She grew up in a predominantly Mexican-American community in Los Angeles and eventually married her Mexican-American high school sweetheart. Nevertheless, she distinctly remembered the importance her family placed on associating with other Chinese:

Q: How important do you think it was to your parents for you to be familiar with Chinese culture?

A: Very important. That you should hang out with Chinese, have Chinese friends. I don't think it was a conscious thing but an underlying thing which puts more pressure. . . . Growing up, yeah it was important. We did all the cultural things, as much as my mother knew.

Q: What did your parents do for work?

A: My father was a postal worker and my mom was a secretary at Cal State L.A. We didn't grow up really "Chinesey." I grew up on pork chops, steak, potatoes, spaghetti. We didn't start eating Chinese food a lot until we got older. It was like 1960s, and it was all Americana. That was what the doctors thought was the best foods to eat and have your kids grow up healthy and strong drinking milk. Now I fight my mom, saying [my kids] don't have to drink that much milk.

Q: Did you eat Chinese food when you were young?

A: We'd only go out for it, into Chinatown. We were a family of five, so we didn't eat out that often. . . . We also, as far as doing Chinese activities, my mom belongs to a Chinese bowling club, and we'd be there every Friday night. My mother and father bowled. All these Chinese people and their Chinese kids and we had these friends at the bowling alley. The only other constant thing growing up that was Chinese was, my mother played mahjong every weekend, either at my aunt's house or my house.

This passage is particularly illuminating for what it says about emerging definitions of culture. By a traditional yardstick, bowling would hardly be considered a Chinese cultural activity, but Karen clearly defines it as such *when it is done with other Chinese.* She grew up understanding that Chinese culture largely rested in associations with other Chinese, and from this perspective, engaging in any activities with other Chinese constitutes a cultural activity.

Once again, the theme of an emergent culture echoing Gary

Hong's earlier observation comes through. Both Gary and Karen were raised to believe that culture ultimately resides within a sense of community and association rather than the ability to speak Chinese or Japanese, practice rituals, or prepare ethnic foods. Our respondents were raised to be believe that associating with coethnics is more important than the actual content of the activity, a theme suggested in Fugita and O'Brien's (1991a) work. From their perspective participating in an ethnic bowling or baseball league, golf club, poker group, fishing club, or even attending a Christian church with a predominantly Asian congregation qualifies as a cultural activity.

"Well, at least date an Asian-American":
Dating and Marriage

Having said all of this, I believe it necessary to reiterate the theme of individual choice discussed earlier. While parents actively encouraged their children to associate with coethnics and Asian-Americans, they ultimately left the choice to them, even concerning issues of dating and marriage. Karen Flores's situation is, once again, illustrative. Despite being highly encouraged to associate with, and by extension, marry a coethnic, she eventually married a Mexican-American. While obviously not their ideal choice for a son-in-law, her parents accepted their union because in the final analysis they believed the choice was hers:

Q: Were their any issues with your family about the marriage?
A: No. I think my mother wished I would marry Chinese until the very end when I got engaged, and once she realized there was no turning back, she came to grips that I'm going to marry a Mexican-American, and that was that.

I heard many stories similar to Karen's, of parents encouraging their childen to marry a coethnic or "at least an Asian-American" but ultimately leaving the choice up to them. Only a few older respondents recalled being given explicit instructions at an early age to only date and eventually marry a coethnic. Morrison Hum, a third-generation Chinese-American in his sixties, described the tone his mother set for him and his siblings early in their lives:

My mother, she did reinforce that, that you are Chinese. I think more so than [I do] with my kids today. Especially with our family, that you marry a Chinese. I heard that a lot. With my sisters and brothers too. So I had that in my mind, maybe subconsciously, that since you are Chinese you marry Chinese. It was difficult [pause] I didn't date any white girls. Mostly all Chinese.

Q: Even though you were in Colorado [for college] and your parents were far away?

A: Right. I did mingle with white kids, both female and male, but didn't date them. I didn't feel comfortable. Maybe I didn't have the self-confidence to do that. It was something, like they were a little higher. When you date, you date an Asian girl, a Chinese especially.

Morrison consciously narrowed his field of potential dating and spousal partners because of the pressures his mother placed on him as well as a belief that white women were out of his league. On this latter point, in many respects white women *were* quite literally out of his league because of antimiscegenation laws throughout the nation.[4]

Such blatant instructions as those that Morrison's mother issued were rare and more likely to be experienced by older respondents. Younger respondents typically sensed their parents' wishes that they marry an Asian since their elders had urged them to associate with coethnics. More often than not, parents couched their feelings in terms of having preferences, such as Kevin Fong's parents:

They specifically set me aside or set us all aside and said for the most part they would be more happy if we were to choose and be with an Asian mate. But they said love conquers all and as long as you're happy. But they kid around. I don't know if they're telling the truth but my Dad said, "If you don't marry an Asian then I'm not going to the wedding" [laugh].

Such examples of subtle manipulation were common. Kevin's parents made clear their bias but acknowledged that the choice was ultimately his to make—"love conquers all." They continued to get their message across by jokingly threatening not to attend his wedding if he chose a non-Asian spouse. If Kevin's current dating patterns are any indication, however, their threats have not influenced his behavior. At the time we interviewed him, Kevin had only dated one Asian woman; the rest were all non-Asian.

Emily Woo, a nonprofit worker in her twenties, was also encouraged to marry a coethnic; however, her mixed Chinese-Japanese heritage complicated the situation. Nevertheless, this did not stop her Japanese-American grandparents from initially encouraging her to marry a coethnic:

> [Mom] married a Chinese man which isn't across race but was a definite no no. Grandma and Grandpa were not happy that she married a Chinese man. So that's part of the reason [Mom] doesn't have a problem with [intermarriages]. Grandma and Grandpa said when growing up, "We are thinking you should marry a nice Japanese boy when you grow up." Like, go to college, get a degree, marry a nice Japanese boy, and have a family. And then she started adding Chinese too because, "Your dad was a nice guy." Then she said white is okay too because, "You'd have cute kids."

Notice how Emily's grandparents gradually expanded the list of suitable spouses. Chinese were eventually deemed acceptable because Emily's mother had already crossed that barrier; Emily, after all, was half Chinese. The change of heart that led to the acceptability of white suitors probably resulted from a combination of factors. First, Emily grew up in a white suburb in northern California. Her grandparents lived nearby and undoubtedly were aware of the limitations of her surroundings. Second, the trend toward intermarriage taking place between white and Japanese ethnics, especially for Sansei, probably softened the idea for her grandparents. With nearly one out of every four native-born Japanese-American women marrying white men, her grandparents had to know this was a distinct possibility for Emily as well. Furthermore, their comment, "You'd have cute kids," says a great deal about how minority group members gradually absorb the dominant group's standards of beauty (Fong & Yung, 1995; Spickard, 1989; Weiss 1973). The prospect of having great-grandchildren with Caucasian influenced features (e.g., rounder eyes and taller physiques) was seen as a good reason to sanction an Asian-white union. While not explicitly stated, some element of hypergamy was also likely involved, such as acknowledging the social advantages accompanying marrying into the dominant group.

"I am the generation that got dragged around": *Lost Cultural Meanings*

Poor intergenerational communication also contributed to weak cultural transmission. In many cases where respondents recalled participating in ethnic rituals or customs as children, the rich meanings behind practices were largely lost because family members failed to make clear why they were performed. Brad Ow, an attorney in his early thirties, remembered a ritual—"brushing the tombs"—he took part in as a boy. Brushing the tombs refers to visiting the burial sites of deceased family members on certain days dictated by the lunar calendar to show respect. A fourth-generation San Franciscan, Brad explained why he no longer carried on the tradition:

> The Chinese stuff that we did, my parents didn't even know the meaning of it. Especially my mom. Obviously my mom knows less than my dad. And so we went out with my dad's grandmother to the cemetery.
>
> *Q:* To brush the tombs?
>
> *A:* Yeah. And every now and then during the year we would go. So I mean, we are the generation that lost that because I would never know what dates to go or what to do. You know, I am the generation that got dragged around. . . . The meaning is lost.

Three strikes work against Brad's continuing participation. First, as an upwardly mobile attorney, Brad is subject to moving where professional opportunities dictate. He had, in fact, only recently returned to San Francisco after having been away for several years. He had simply not been there to participate. Second, in order to participate he has to rely on his family to inform him of the specific dates since he cannot interpret the lunar calendar. Last, and perhaps most significant, the ritual is largely devoid of sacred meaning to Brad because no one has ever clearly explained to him why it is performed or what needs to be done. His childhood memories of the ritual involve running around the cemetery grounds and playing with his siblings while family members "did their thing." Note here as well Brad's comment that even his parents "didn't know the meaning" behind the ritual. Brad's immigrant grandparents on his father's side were the driving force behind carrying on the tradition while his second-generation father and third-generation mother looked on.

We heard many stories similar to Brad's, of customs practiced during childhood being discarded in adulthood because the reasons for observing were never clearly explained. While in the past communication between the generations may also have been poor, at least larger structural supports enforced participation in cultural activities. Community members risked severe social sanctions if they attempted to rebel. Today, geographic dispersion brought on by occupational restructuring and suburbanization have changed all of that (Yancey et al., 1976). Individuals are now free to discard or retain whatever cultural elements they choose without fear of negative sanction—even a parent's guilt stings less when separated by hundreds or thousands of miles.

Daphne Kitano, a Yonsei in her twenties, provides another example of this process of cultural shedding:

> The main thing was New Year's. My mom makes a lot of traditional Japanese foods, and the biggest celebration is New Year's morning with this big breakfast and foods we only have once a year. . . . We also got this little (pause) I don't know what it's called, in fact I don't even really know what it symbolizes. I think it's supposed to be good luck for the new year. Like it's a couple of rice cakes and then there's a piece of *kobu*, the seaweed, topped with a tangerine. I don't know what it [pause] I used to think it was a snowman [laugh] but it symbolizes something like fortune or I forget what. I'll have to ask my mom again.

Now an adult with her own apartment, Daphne has not carried on the New Year's tradition of arranging rice cakes and seaweed. Nor does it seem likely that when she marries and has children, she will teach them this ritual because of her own confusion over what the "snowman" represents. The practice holds no sacred meaning to her beyond the sentimental feelings she attaches to it as part of her childhood memories. This problem of lost meaning behind traditional events and rituals has been well documented in the white ethnic experience (Alba, 1990; Gans, 1979; Waters, 1990). Apparently, the same problem plagues Asian ethnics as well.

Not being able to hold conversations with immigrant grandparents also contributed to poor cultural communication for our third-generation respondents. Since grandparent and grandchild carried on only the most rudimentary of conversations, rich opportunities for cultural transmission and learning were effectively lost. In the process, an important link to a living cultural repository was severed. Grandparents were unable to share details of the villages or towns they came from, of their lives before coming to the United States, or to teach cultural lessons through ethnic stories and fairy tales. Paula Inouye shared her sorrow over her inability to share with her grandparents:

Q: Did your grandparents teach you about Japanese culture?
A: No, because there was a language barrier. I missed having that kind of a relationship. All I remember to me, as grandparents, was somebody that [pause] they would come and give us like money and treats and in broken English they would say, "Oh, you good child."

Barry Sato, a Sansei in his forties, also shared memories of his grandfather who eventually moved into his parents' home:

My grandfather on my mom's side lived with us for a couple of years, but I didn't see him that much because I was [pause] it was the last year of high school and the first few years of college. So obviously, a senior in high school so you are never home and when you are in college you are in and out. Really, the last year, the second year in college, he went to Japan, and he died in Japan. He was funny because I would call home to say I was going to be late, and he would say, "Not home. Click." He was a very good man, a very gentle man. I wish I had known him better. Going back, this is what I learned from my uncle. My grandfather wanted his kids, the Nisei, to be American citizens, to learn English and everything else.

This passage captures the bittersweet price the first generation paid to fulfill its immigrant dreams. By encouraging his progeny to become bona fide American citizens, Barry's grandfather unintentionally assured his estrangement from his own grandchildren. He died proud of his children and grandchildren's successes but was unable to express his feelings fully or share his own experiences with them.

"In their era they were only picking and choosing the pieces of the Chinese culture that would work in their America": Intentional Reasons

As we have seen, there were numerous unintentional reasons why cultural transmission was weak between respondents and their families. Intentional reasons also played a factor. Some families chose not to uphold cultural traditions or values they saw as incongruent with their lifestyles. Frank Wu shared his thoughts on his parents' attitudes:

Q: How important was it for your parents to make you familiar with Chinese culture?

A: I would say very. It seems like a matter of course that you were expected to know the customs and be schooled in them and be part of it. The customs, the ethic. Not so much the filial piety because in some way they felt, okay, they were trapped in it and pursued it, but they felt there was a lot of bad things in it too. Too much looking inward to the family and commitment and not enough, as my dad would call it, "progress." Because he was a modern guy too. There was always this schizophrenia going on. Healthy schizophrenia. In their era they were only picking and choosing the pieces of the Chinese culture that would work in their America.

I was struck here by the similarity between Frank's insights into his parents' behavior and a recent article by Nagel (1994) on the social construction of ethnicity. She writes:

It is important that we discard the notion that culture is simply an historical legacy; culture is *not* a shopping cart that comes to us already loaded with a set of historical cultural goods. Rather, we construct culture by picking and choosing items from the shelves of the past and the present. (p. 162)

The two passages neatly complement one another since both highlight the notion of personal agency in cultural construction.

Others responded to the strong pressures they felt to Americanize and purposefully sought rapid acculturation to avoid racial hostility. Japanese ethnics as well as older Chinese ethnics, in particular, recalled the messages they received from their families to assimilate. Chuck Hayashi, a high school counselor in his forties, described the cues he picked up from his family while growing up:

> We did the American things. I've never really asked them [why]. I think it might have been because they felt if we were going to have the chance to fit in we needed to be more like the majority and not be real different. . . .
>
> Q: Do you think you've lost [touch with] your Japanese culture?
> A: Yeah, probably, but I don't think I ever had it. I didn't lose it. I was just never given something that wasn't only connected through bloodline or ancestry. I don't think I'm missing anything. I would like to know more about it, but I've always felt I'd rather visit other parts of the U.S. than Japan.

In the aftermath of World War Two, Japanese-American families experienced very real demands to Americanize and prove themselves to be good citizens. While Chinese-Americans also suffered from nativist fears and felt pressured to assimilate, Japanese-Americans experienced heightened pressures, both internally and externally generated, resulting from being singled out for internment. Such pressures effectively stifled cultural expression for many Japanese-American families. Chris Takeuchi, a Sansei in her forties, was particularly eloquent on this point:

> I don't think [passing on Japanese culture] was that important to them at all. I think like many Nisei neither of them had ever talked about their wartime experiences. And it was only on my urging and questions asked during the '60s when most of us were involved in the movement that they started talking about it. I think racially they were always very proud

that they were Japanese, and they felt that I should also be very proud to be Japanese, but it was much more in a sense of identity and a sense of pride rather than doing things that were Japanese, you know, or eating things. There was never a point made in doing things that were primarily Japanese. I think there was an assumption and a hope that I would marry someone who was Japanese. Things like that. . . . I think like so many Nisei they were in this postwar era and were very concerned about proving to everyone else that they were American. And I think a lot of Nisei set out to prove that they were 110 percent American and to basically prove that the wartime incarceration was wrong.

In *The Legacy of Injustice* (1993), Donna Nagata discusses the tension many Japanese-American families felt because of the war to be "super" Americans. One major impact of internment was the minimization of "behaviors related to Japanese-American culture" (p.137). Survivors of the camp experience, such as Chuck's and Chris's parents, made the conscious decision to do "American things" and be 110 percent American to maximize their chances for fitting in and succeeding. They purposefully did not raise their children to follow traditional cultural practices, believing that to acculturate as quickly as possible would be better in the long run.

Peggy Endo's mother adopted this strategy in raising her family. A Sansei in her forties, Peggy described her efforts to make life easier for her children:

She did everything she thought she should do as a good citizen. I mean, I don't think she ever missed an election. She volunteered to do things even though she worked a lot. Like she volunteered for things at school, and I remember she was a scout leader for Girl Scouts. She did everything she could to make it easier for us. I mean like the kids.

Q: You mean as far as adjusting?

A: Yeah, I think so. I mean it was really important. . . . For her to be accepted you had to be a part of society. You couldn't just sit back and like not participate. She was always very community oriented. More so than my father.

Peggy's mother wanted desperately to be seen as a loyal American, a patriot, and a contributor to her community. She understood that being Japanese meant she and her family were suspect and thus already had strikes against them. While ultimately powerless to influence other people's perceptions of her, becoming a scout leader, volunteering at school, and otherwise being community oriented allowed Peggy's mother to feel better about herself and more useful to her family.

Another way parents tried to make life easier for their children was by giving them Anglicized names. Meg Takahashi, a Sansei in her thirties, described how her parents decided to name her:

> [I] was given an American first name and this was for assimilation purposes so I would not have trouble and be ridiculed in grammar school. And when I was younger and it was pretty cool until, you know, my middle name was Akiko, and then they said what is that and stuff, and it was really unusual at that time. Everyone had names like Kathy, John, and David and middle names were about the same.

Meg's parents consciously decided to suppress their Japanese heritage in naming their daughter. By giving Meg an Anglicized first name, they hoped to mitigate the perception of foreignness that might otherwise plague her.

Having said all of this, I do not wish to leave the impression that respondents who grew up feeling pressure to acculturate were also encouraged to break away from the ethnic community. On the contrary, we have seen that respondents were encouraged by their families to seek out coethnics for friendship. What is important to note about these friendships, however, is that most were not ethnically centered. That is, the activities they engaged in, discussions they had, and so forth, were not centered around ethnic themes. They were encouraged to live an American lifestyle but to do so with other Asian-Americans.

Gordon's (1964) notion of structural pluralism is significant here. He noted that though major religious and racial groups have acculturated to mainstream cultural norms, they, nevertheless, have remained structurally separate outside the workplace, maintaining their own communal institutions, cliques, and networks of friends. While the reasons for this involved both voluntary (self-segregation) and involuntary (racism and discrimination) forces, the outcome was parallel communities, all highly acculturated but distinct. It seems this was the model most of our respondents were raised to aspire to.

▨ *"You gotta work twice as hard": Family Discussions about Racism and Discrimination*

In light of what has been said so far about the pressures some felt to assimilate and the racial and cultural intolerance underlying those pressures, the question of whether their families openly discussed racism and discrimination comes to mind. And here the Asian ethnics we spoke with diverge from the literature on white ethnics. About one fourth of our respondents recalled that as children they had talked with family members about racism and discrimination. Most of these discussions involved retelling incidents that had happened to family members, of thwarted careers, and being warned to "watch out" in their own lives. For example, Laura Nee's grandfather, because he was Chinese, could not find work despite being a third-generation American with a college degree. He shared his bitter experience with his children and grandchildren:

> My dad's dad spoke fluent English and went to the University of Chicago and got a degree in engineering, although he ended up having to take over his dad's store. He couldn't find work. They wouldn't hire him.
>
> Q: Did he express bitterness?
> A: Yes he did. He was bitter, and he also, because of that, he refused to speak English although he spoke it fluently, perfect English.
> Q: Not even with the grandkids?
> A: No. Always Chinese.

The memory of her grandfather being denied the opportunity to work in his chosen profession because of racism left an indelible mark on Laura. As she described to me later, her grandfather's warning to "watch out" resonated deeply for her because of how racism had so clearly affected the direction his own life had taken.

Others recalled being warned they needed to work harder to

achieve their goals because they were not white. Both Frank Wu's and Chuck Hayashi's parents sat them down to discuss the reality of power relations and racial dynamics in the United States. To get ahead as a member of a minority group, their parents counseled, they needed to put in much more effort:

Frank: [My parents] also instilled in me the fact that you never were quite completely equal. In our era, we were always warned and reminded, like I'm sure that you *are not*, that you gotta work twice as hard, perform twice as well, because in order to be equal you had to be twice as good. Today, I don't know how you all feel about it. I don't think the deep-seated prejudices have totally gone away. They are still there. I think the tragedy of it is that most young people, even yourselves as students today, you don't sense it, don't discover it, you don't feel it, until perhaps it is too late for your lives. You'll discover it when you are working for someone, and you want that director's job and you don't get it, or a plum opportunity overseas and you don't get it. You begin to wonder why, and you might not even know why for some time.

Chuck: [Racism] never tore me up, but what helped me was just little things my parents used to tell me. Like, yes, you are different, but the people that really count will overlook things like that. My dad would say things like that. But he would also say, look, you are a minority, and you will have to compete for jobs and things with the majority. And he would tell me. I know it was to make me work harder because he would say we have to do twice as good to get the jobs. He told me that several times.

Frank chided his interviewer, a Chinese-American male in his twenties, for not being more watchful of racism because early on it was drilled in him to be alert at all times. In his eyes, "young people" today have let down their guard and become complacent, thereby leaving themselves vulnerable to tremendous disappointment later in life, for example, when they are passed over for a "plum opportunity."

Lorraine Ito, a Sansei in her forties, was raised to be fearful of non-Japanese and to expect poor treatment:

> I think my father made me feel there was prejudice more than other people made me feel it. You know what I mean? Like when I was at Park Village Elementary School, we were the only Japanese at the school, but the teachers liked us. I got along really well with the people and the teachers. So I don't remember feeling any prejudice there. I always did well in school, or thought I did well. I never thought my race had anything to do with it. I think I was more self-conscious of being Japanese because my father had said that, had pointed out that I was different, but I don't think other people made me feel like that. I don't ever remember feeling like that.

Later, Lorraine came to understand that her parents' distrust of non-Japanese was rooted in their wartime internment experience. The harsh treatment they had received left a damaging impression on them and eroded their sense of security. Whites were not to be trusted and the best strategy to avoid problems was to maintain a low profile and stay with one's own kind. They, in turn, passed on their fears and suspicions to their children:

> It was very important to my parents for us to meet Japanese people and to only go out with Japanese people, do things with Japanese people. They didn't even like it if . . . They didn't mind me having Caucasian girlfriends, but they didn't like it if any boys came by and visited. Even just friends stopped by. They wanted us to only socialize with just Japanese boys.
>
> Q: Why is that?
>
> A: I didn't know it at the time but I think [pause] my mother was in the camp, but she never told us about camp. It was like an embarrassing situation for her, so they never discussed camp with us at all. And because she went to camp, and my father was sent to Idaho, they felt that the Japanese people were singled out. So growing up one of the things that really sticks in my mind was my father telling me you have to do everything everyone tells you. Like at school, you have to behave. You cannot stick out like a sore thumb because even if there's a group of people, I have black hair and dark eyes and slanted eyes, and so I'm Japanese, and I

will be pointed out before the Caucasian people. And I didn't know why he said it. I found out later that it probably had to do with feelings about having to be sent away or relocate.

Q: Did you believe him?

A: Yes. Yeah, so I always wanted to behave. I think that made me very insecure. . . . I think I didn't feel real real comfortable around the Caucasian people. I think I felt inferior. Somewhat inferior and then I think I gravitated to Japanese people. After meeting them, I gravitated to them because they were just like me. They liked the same food I did. They thought like me. And those are the friends we stay in contact with.

As we can see, the picture that Lorraine's parents painted had a significant influence not only on her sense of safety and self-worth but on her actions as well. As Osajima (1993) argues, Lorraine had internalized the distrust and anxiety her father developed as a result of his painful experiences with racism. Even after coming to her own more optimistic conclusions about non-Japanese, Lorraine continued to feel a sense of comfort with coethnics, a reaction that she recognized came from her earlier insecurities. Today, she continues to feel more comfortable with coethnic friends.

We can also observe the roots of a collective strategy that many Asian-Americans use to get by in a racist society—stay quiet, behave, and hope that nobody bothers you. This strategy makes sense in many ways, yet the costs associated with it are steep. Certainly on the surface being characterized as a quiet, "model" minority seems much better than being stereotyped as a lazy or welfare-dependent minority group. The price paid for behaving and being obedient, however, is that you are not taken seriously because those in power expect acquiescence. Thus the model minority is not expected to complain or raise any fuss even when clear abuse is present.

"They just talk about it like it was nothing": Family
Communication about the Wartime Internment
of Japanese-Americans

Understandably for the Japanese ethnics we interviewed, family discussions about racism invariably touched upon the wartime internment experience. In Lorraine's case, what was communicated to her was the need to use caution in dealing with non-Japanese. She was not alone in this respect. Other Japanese respondents also recalled family members sharing accounts of the indignities they faced. Dale Fujimoto, a Sansei in his forties, was urged by his father to protect himself by getting a good education:

> [I]t's true that the Nisei . . . were a lot more affected by the internment, so they got a late start on their careers. . . . My father graduated from U.C.L.A. in 1944 and he couldn't find a job. He had to go back to work on the farm. There's nothing wrong with that, but that's just the way it was back then. He was told that there was a sudden threatening war with Japan. He suffered from that prejudice and lack of opportunity was common for the Niseis, second generation. . . . I think we were aware of the fact that we were different because I remember my father telling me that it was important to get an education because it's something they can't take away from you. And I remember asking him what that meant, and he said because the Japanese-American community had gone to camp, they had lost everything, and the only reason they were able to start again was because they had an education.

Tracy Nagata also recalled hearing about her grandfather and father's experiences when she was a child:

> [M]y paternal grandfather talked about racism during World War Two because sometimes he would be stopped and ID'ed just because he was Japanese and Pearl Harbor, and he was really pissed off about that. . . . For my dad it wasn't so much camp because he was a year old and probably two when he left. He talked about how on December 7 he'd get rocks thrown at him or beaten up. People saying, "Oh you Jap!"

Tracy spoke with bitterness when she recounted this story. Now a young woman in her twenties and pursuing a graduate degree in Asian-American studies, she has not forgotten the pain or anger conveyed to her when she first heard these accounts.

Then there were others who grew up in families where talk

about internment was avoided altogether. Diane Okihiro's parents and grandparents were all interned but did not voluntarily discuss this aspect of their lives with her:

> I didn't know anything about the camps and stuff until the museum went up and they started to ask my grandparents for artifacts. And then I started taking classes and started learning probably what my parents went through, and I started asking them questions, and then I would kind of learn a little bit. But before then I didn't know anything. They don't talk about it. You're not supposed to talk about stuff like that. You just don't. It's like, why bother, it's over with. Kind of let it go, type of thing.

Diane's experience was common. More often than not, family members did not discuss either their internment experience at all or only mentioned it in passing. Chris Takeuchi discussed the matter-of-fact way her parents referred to their experience:

> I think I always knew they went to camp, but it was all sort of in passing: "Well, you know during the war we were put in camp." But I didn't really know what that meant, and it wasn't really until I went to college that I made a point of learning about it, you know, reading some books, you know, that answered questions.

In accounting for the silence maintained about a period so significant in their lives, Nagata (1993) suggests that denial and the repression of painful memories, guilt and shame, and a wish to protect younger generations from the past discouraged family discussions. She also points to the communication style characterizing interactions between the generations: "Whether the Nisei purposefully refrained from talking about the camps for whatever reasons, their perceived style of cryptic and/or matter-of-fact communications led many Sansei to avoid asking further questions" (pp. 101–102). Often not until many years later did family members finally open up and share their memories, usually at the prompting of their children or in response to the Reparations Movement. Kanji Furuye,

They were proud of their heritage but talked good of the United States. Even after the camps I didn't hear the bitterness. It wasn't until I grew up and started to ask questions that they let out a little bit of the bitterness that they had inside of them. I think they didn't want their kids to have that bad mentality. I look back at old Christmas pictures, and I see my brother with so many presents and [comparing] myself at the same age, I got a pair of socks. And when I would ask why, they would always tell me that it was lost in the war, and they were making up for it. And that's about all I've ever heard from them.

▨ *Summary*

In many respects, the Asian ethnics we interviewed "fit" the major findings drawn about white ethnics and their childhood experiences. Growing up, they were not expected to rigidly adhere to traditional cultural practices or values. Instead, what was emphasized was the importance of developing an appreciation of their hyphenated identities and the emergent cultural values and practices of their parents' generation. Foremost of these was the importance of associating with coethnics and/or other Asian-Americans regardless of the content of the activity. Therefore, Asian-American baseball Little Leagues, Boy/Girl Scout troops, and basketball tournaments were all seen as appropriate and legitimate outlets for cultural sharing. In this respect, our respondents' experiences growing up differ somewhat from those of white ethnics. Their parents placed more importance on coethnic and pan-Asian associations compared to white ethnic parents. Given their small numbers compared to whites, their parents needed to take more proactive measures to ensure ethnic association.

Our respondents' childhood experiences differed from white ethnics in one other important aspect. Their parents were more likely to warn them about the harmful consequences of racism and discrimination and to discuss the realities of being a minority in a majority white society. These warnings had the effect of producing a sense of wariness for some in their dealings with non-Asians. I would describe this wariness as the need for vigilance, to keep one's guard up for protection. While clearly not the case for all of our respondents, the fact that a quarter did grow up with this sense of caution stands as a departure from the white ethnic experience. Whites might vaguely recall or assume that an ancestor experienced prejudice sometime in the past, but for Asian ethnics the memories are still quite fresh and therefore salient (Waters, 1990, p. 97).

"I knew that I was different"
Childhood Neighborhood Influences

It is well known that childhood experiences often set the stage for the development of a salient ethnic identity in later life. Clearly, the role of the family in this process is pivotal. Parents and kin, after all, establish precedent for the foods prepared, language(s) spoken, customs observed, and importance placed on coethnic friendships. However, parents influence their children's ethnic development in another important way as well. Where they choose to raise their children can profoundly shape their lives by circumscribing the population(s) they have daily contact with. The demographics of their community and outlying areas largely influence whether children experience much or little prejudice and discrimination, have opportunities to explore their cultural heritage outside the family, and are encouraged either to be proud of their heritage or to shun it.

Through interactions with friends and strangers outside the home, young people develop a sense of themselves separate from how their families see them within the home. In the realms of the classroom and schoolyard, the neighborhood, and community, they learn what meanings their race and ethnicity hold for the larger society by watching how others respond to these aspects of their identity. They learn, in short, how salient their ethnicity and race are to others. With this information, they begin to decide whether these aspects of their identity are their own private affair or whether society has an interest in them.

As we began to explore our respondents' childhood experiences outside the home, many differences dependent on neighborhood composition emerged. Respondents raised in predominantly white communities struggled to various degrees with issues of marginalization based on their racial background. Those who grew up in Asian-centered communities, in contrast, described race as largely a "nonissue" since others around them were also Asian. The experiences of respondents raised in racially diverse neighborhoods varied depending on the particular demographic combination and history of their community. While some regarded race and ethnicity as highly permeable boundaries, others had a completely different experience where not only racial, but ethnic distinctions were clearly drawn. Below is a review of each of these combinations.

"Am I really that different?": Growing Up Asian in a Predominantly White Neighborhood

A little more than a third of our respondents grew up in predominantly white suburban communities; all were under the age of fifty but most were less than thirty, reflecting in part the legacy of racist housing policies that, until recently, successfully segregated Asian-American families. Most of these neighborhoods were in California, typically bedroom communities outside San Francisco and in the Los Angeles area.[1] Except for a few Japanese ethnics who grew up in farming communities that were transformed into suburban tracts, no one claimed to have extensive ties to their neighborhood. Typically, their families had moved in after they were born. The reasons recalled for relocation were similar—as their parents achieved greater economic security, they sought superior housing, quality schools, and greater social standing. Suburban communities satisfied all of these demands.

Those who lived only in white neighborhoods during their adolescence described their childhood as "ordinary" and shared memories of playing with other children in the neighborhood, riding bikes up and down the block, and selling lemonade in the summer. As Emily Woo recalled, "I went right from the hospital to Orinda and led a sheltered, uneventful life."

Nevertheless, when comparing their lives with those of their white friends and schoolmates, Emily and others also remembered the not-so-ordinary aspects of childhood, the painful moments that both stereotyping and intentional prejudice caused. Stereotyping, while not intentionally meant to alienate or offend, occurred more frequently. For example, many recalled being the first and sometimes only Asian family to live in the neighborhood and subsequently being treated as representatives of their race and culture. Meg Takahashi was viewed as an expert on Japanese culture despite being a third-generation Japanese-American:

> It was very frank. There would be questions people would ask who obviously had never been exposed to the Japanese culture. So they would ask me like in high school if I ate sitting on the floor, if I only ate Japanese food, did I eat any American food, and a typical question would be, do I only speak Japanese at home.

Moments of awkwardness and feeling out of place occured as when Stan Hifumi, a Sansei in his late thirties, played spin the bottle with a group of friends: "Whenever it was my turn to spin, none of the [white] girls wanted to kiss the Japanese guy." Tony Lam, a teacher in his forties and of Chinese and Japanese ancestry, experienced similar tensions as a teenager, only in his case he felt pressure to date the only Asian girl in school:

> I was the only Asian boy going to that school, and I knew that because when I was looking for a date actually, I didn't choose it, my friends did. My friends were Caucasian, and I remember saying to my friend George, who do I take the dance, the ninth grade dance . . . and he stands up and looks back at the last girl in my row and that's Susan Lee, and I'm thinking, oh no, not her, but because he's playing around with his eyes, I felt the pressure like, okay, I'm now obliged to take her because she looks like me, but my preference is Caucasian girls.

Tony's friend assumed that because he was Asian, he should *naturally* date the Asian girl despite his own preference for Caucasian girls. While expressed without hostility, the message Tony clearly got from his friend was the familiar adage, "stick with your own kind."

Sometimes their "Japaneseness" or "Chineseness" became salient in the classroom. These moments usually occurred during social studies lessons when they were called upon, usually by a teacher, as an expert on Chinese or Japanese culture. Awkward moments were also recalled during history lessons. Japanese ethnics such as Paula Inouye, a Sansei in her mid-forties, particularly felt uncomfortable during discussions about the Second World War: "I remember in the fifth grade also when they started talking about the bombing of Pearl Harbor, and I felt really self-conscious then, like, that's my race, you know. I didn't do anything about it, but I felt really self-conscious." Paula later confided that her self-consciousness stemmed from her fear of being seen as foreign, "not American," by her white peers.

Virtually everyone who grew up in a white community recalled incidents of intentional prejudice as well. These ranged from racial slurs and teasing to physical fights and discriminatory treatment. An incident could happen anywhere: the playground, the neighborhood street, a restaurant, the schoolyard, a public bathroom. And it could be started by anyone: a friend during an argument, a stranger on the street or driving by in a car, a store clerk, schoolmates. Some discounted these incidents as the acts of ignorant people despite recounting many "individual acts" in order to protect their self-esteem. Others, however, felt the full sting of their adolescent tormentors. Tony Lam,

> Sometimes I thought I should just die. I thought, gee, I thought I caused so much problems. All I got is this, you know, and so at times I looked in the mirror and I go, gee, I looked Asian but I eat their food, dance their dance, I read English, am I really that different? But because they assign so much to differences, they go by outward difference than what counts. We learn to hate people who are different and that's not [because of] anything that I did. . . . They never [knew] me. So how do

I feel? I feel more than I can explain if I could, but it turned out to be self-hatred. . . . I grew up hating myself. I was a no good lousy Jap. But I never hated Japanese. I never did.

This poignant passage captures the pain Tony felt in his youth as a result of internalizing the racism of others (Osajima, 1993). It also reveals the historical specificity of the racism he experienced since, having grown up in the 1950s, he had to deal with the legacy of the Second World War. Despite being of both Chinese and Japanese ancestry, Tony referred to himself as a "lousy Jap" because that was how his tormentors saw him. Reflecting years later, he spoke with chagrin about how he could have handled the episode differently: "You know what's funny is, and . . . this hit later in high school, I thought to myself, I should have told them when I was in my youth, like elementary, if I had the wherewithal, 'No, I'm not a Jap, I'm Chinese.' Isn't that ironic?"

Some racist incidents were age specific. Residential discrimination, for example, was only mentioned by those over the age of forty. Frequently mentioned experiences included petitions circulated to gauge neighborhood sentiment, sellers who refused to sell to their family, and racist real estate agents. Chris Takeuchi recalled the difficulties her family encountered when they tried to move:

> When we were thinking about moving at one point when I was in elementary school [pause] some of the places that we went to look to move we were told in kind of indirect terms that they wouldn't sell to us because we were [pause] or we weren't white.
> *Q:* How did this make you feel?
> *A:* Well, that was the first time I felt or I had heard, really, that it was with adults and that it actually really existed. I think I was aware of it primarily because, primarily as a sort of more white-black polarity kind of thing. I didn't really figure Asians in it. And because there were so many other whites around, I never really considered myself any different. But then when there was such overt discrimination in not being able to buy in certain areas, it became very apparent.

Chris was caught off guard by the fact that housing discrimination "actually really existed." Up to that point in her life she had not considered how her "Asianness" affected the way people might treat her or her family because she believed racial tensions were confined between blacks and whites—"I didn't really figure Asians in it." In effect, she saw herself as having an honorary status having grown up around whites without much conflict. This episode altered her sense of security and opened her eyes to another reality.

▨ *"I think I just tried to manage": Moving into Predominantly White Neighborhoods*

In contrast to respondents who lived in white communities all their lives were those who moved from predominantly Asian or racially mixed neighborhoods. The alienation this group experienced was particularly intense since they had memories of a very different experience before moving. Tracy Nagata, who moved to San Jose from Hawaii in her teens, was particularly eloquent on this topic:

> I grew up knowing what it was like to grow up dominant in society, and I saw my community playing big roles in society and government. I grew up in a part of Honolulu which was 90 percent Japanese-American . . . and in terms of food, you get all kinds of things. At McDonald's you could have rice, so you could definitely tell the Asian influence that was there. . . . But when I was fourteen, I moved to California, West San Jose, which was like really white. I went from a junior high that was 90 percent Asian or people of color, to a high school that was the opposite.

Lynn Jong, a third-generation Chinese-American in her forties, also recalled moving at a young age from a predominantly Chinese community in Fresno to a white community across town. She discussed how the move affected her self-esteem:

> You look at my kindergarten picture, and there were like a couple whites, and most were nonwhite. And you go to my first grade picture, and me and one other Chicano, a Mexican kid, was in the picture, and the rest were white. So that was the biggest contrast. So it did something to me. I think it made

me insecure because I was very self-conscious of how I was physically. That I was different, physically, from everybody else.

Respondents such as Lynn and Tracy who recalled an earlier community where they were "just like everybody else" vividly remembered the awkwardness and sense of loss they felt upon moving into a white neighborhood. As children they wished they did not feel so different which, when probed to elaborate, often meant they had wished they were not Chinese or Japanese. Being Chinese or Japanese in effect meant not being "normal" in the eyes of their white peers.

The question, "Why me?" came up a number of times as they struggled to make sense of the pain and confusion they felt in being singled out. Sharon Young, a fourth-generation Chinese-American in her twenties, described how being racially different compounded the loneliness of being a newcomer:

> I think I was pretty very conscious [of being Chinese] because of being called names and prejudice, and I used to think it's unfair, like, "Why am I this color? How come people used to make fun of you, and you didn't do anything wrong?" I mean, I think it was really sad to have to go through that adjustment, 'cause moving is just a hard enough thing, to move to a new area, when you're settled there. But then to also experience people calling you names and things. You feel very left out. I felt very left out when I was in school. I used to kinda like hang out by myself and try to avoid certain people that I thought would make fun of me.

Harsh treatment (bullying, rock and bottle throwing, vandalism, etc.) or teasing from their white peers usually caused such feelings. Bill Saito, a Yonsei in his late twenties, for example, recalled moving from an area of West Los Angeles where a vital Japanese-American community resided, to Agoura Hills, which at the time was a new housing development with few minorities. For Bill, the physical move was not nearly as difficult or confusing as the psychological shift it demanded. His experience upon moving to Agoura Hills, while extreme in its effect, is illustrative.

Q: What do you remember about moving to Agoura?

A: Yeah, well, when I first got there I didn't like it. . . . I think school I didn't like . . . because you get picked on. We were bused into the [San Fernando] Valley because there were no schools out there and so I would get picked on. I didn't like that.

Q: What kind of picking?

A: Racial stuff. . . . There were racial slurs all the time ranging from X to your ethnicity even to slurs on other ethnicities that you kinda look like but they don't mean the same thing to you . . . chink or kimchee or whatever else.

Q: How did that make you feel at the time?

A: Well, I think I developed colitis from it. Yeah, it's brought on by stress. It's the inflammation of your stomach. Kinda like an ulcer, and it persisted through the time I was in fifth grade before they actually . . . and then in fifth grade it got *really* bad, and I was out of school for like a whole week. And they took me to a doctor, and the first time he diagnosed it as appendicitis, so they took it out, and it wasn't even my appendix. And then it flared back up as soon as I hit junior high.

Those similar to Bill who moved into white neighborhoods spoke with unusual clarity about the distress they experienced in adjusting to their new surroundings and their struggles to gain acceptance. In Bill's case he literally swallowed the prejudice and racism directed at him and, as a result, developed an ulcer-like condition at a ridiculously young age.

"We made it so we could make our friends laugh":
The Strategy of Self-mockery

Respondents used a variety of strategies to deal with their sense of racial marginalization, one of which involved self mockery. Jerry Fong, a fourth-generation Chinese-American in his early twenties and brother of Kevin Fong, described his survival strategy for fitting in when his family moved to San Dimas:

[I]n San Dimas I think it was brought up, and it was pointed out that I was Chinese, and though I wanted so much to be like the majority, I was different. Especially [pause] I was joked at. I was joked about driving, about just stereotypical Asian things [pause] using chopsticks, "Konichiwa." I mean those things that people bring up when they lump you as an Asian into this huge, large stereotypical category. And that's when I knew I was Chinese. . . . [My brother and] I played football throughout my high school years, and that really influenced my friends, and there weren't many Asians at all. . . . So you know when Ronald Reagan was president, they used to say, "One for the gipper," right? And so they would say, "Why don't you do one for the nipper," and stuff like that. But the funny thing was that it was a joke by us. We made it so we could make our friends laugh, so stuff like that happened. And I remember an incident where I went up to a counter at a pizza parlor, and just to make my friends laugh, I'd ask the guy behind the counter, "Hey do you have any chopsticks?" And it's so degrading now that I think about it, but at the time it was okay.

This passage poignantly captures the dilemma some found themselves in after moving to a predominantly white neighborhood. Because he did not feel secure about being Chinese in his new setting, Jerry believed he needed to mock himself, "beat them to the punch," to gain acceptance by his white peers. His strategy worked, but at great psychological cost. Jerry ultimately knew that what he was doing was demeaning to himself, insulting to other Asians, and perpetuating stereotypes about Asians, nevertheless he felt compelled to carry on with his behavior despite its damaging effects. At the time, the immediate relief he felt from disarming his white peers justified any longterm consequences he would pay for humiliating himself.

Students in Stacey Lee's (1996) study of Asian-American youth spoke of using the same self-mocking strategy in order to make themselves less threatening to their white friends. To get by in their social world, some students believed to get on the good side of their white peers, which meant playing the jokester role at their own expense, was essential. On the surface these students were well liked, as Jerry believed himself to be. And yet, the price paid for gaining acceptance reflects what Osajima (1993) refers to as the hidden injuries of race; they paid with their self-dignity.

Later on in the interview, Jerry described an incident that happened while on a family outing that showed the fallacies of his strategy:

> I remember one incident in L.A. Well, many, many times throughout my life I remember people just passing by doing the "ying, ying, yong" thing, just the way people think that Asians speak. Specifically one time, it was my parents, our family was at Pizza Hut. There was this white guy, I bet he was like twenty years old, with his friend, and he passed by us, and he said the same thing. And he said it so basically the whole family could hear, and I felt uncomfortable. I wanted to kick some ass, but I was a little kid. And at the time you don't know how to react, you don't know what to do. I mean, it's like a disgrace to your whole family, you know, this guy is making a disgrace to your whole family. You're supposed to fight for them. If someone messes with your family, you're supposed to mess with them back. But as a child, I didn't know how to react at the time.

Jerry had devised a way to get along in the company of his schoolmates, but amid strangers there was no way to ensure against mistreatment. Surprise "attacks" or bouts of prejudice and discrimination caught folks like Jerry off guard, leaving them unsure about how to react. Invariably, however, feelings of confusion, anger and shame surfaced in the aftermath of an incident.

Understandably, some respondents with stories similar to Jerry's admitted these experiences left them distrustful of whites. Marie Nishida, a Sansei in her forties,

> People used to throw rocks at me, call Jap, you know, little boys when I walked home from school. So I knew I was different.
>
> *Q:* How did that make you feel?
>
> *A:* Pretty bad, you know, it's no fun. And at that time it was like the TV fare was all these World War Two movies, right, so it would be like, "Kill the Jap! Kill the Jap!" . . . When we were living there, I think I just tried to manage. I think what happened was I developed kind of a basic mistrust of white people. . . . My grandfather had a nursery. He had the land up there for, way before, I mean,

you know, hardly anything in town. And then, meanwhile, the neighborhood had grown up around the nursery, so we were going to move onto the nursery land and build a house. The neighborhood tried to petition us out.

Having been mistreated at an early age by her white peers and neighbors, Marie learned she needed to be cautious when interacting with whites. Her family later moved to West Los Angeles where there were more Japanese-Americans like herself, but the sting of being abused in her former neighborhood lingered: "And so when we went to West L.A. there was a pretty big group being, not huge, but to me it was big because it was more than I'd ever been with at school of Japanese, and they couldn't understand me because I left there hating white people."

I am not suggesting here that all respondents who moved into white neighborhoods suffered from the same difficulties as Jerry or Bill or developed the same degree of mistrust as Marie, nor am I suggesting that those who grew up in white neighborhoods from the start did not experience similar stress. What I am suggesting is that these respondents could articulate their feelings of hurt more clearly because they had a point of reference to compare their current experiences with. They experienced a sense of loss in addition to a general sense of marginalization.

"I guess in a way it's like assimilating": The Strategy of Avoidance and Diverting Attention Away from One's "Asianness"

Not surprisingly, few Asian-Americans, a small handful at best, attended the same schools as respondents who grew up in white communities. Sara Lo, a third-generation Chinese-American in her late forties who grew up in San Bernardino, recalled her experiences:

When I first went to grade school it was mostly white. I don't remember any other Asians in grade school. . . . In junior high school, again, mostly whites and there was one other Asian boy who was my brother Dan's age who was at that junior high and then high school.

Q: Did you two seek out the other Asians in school?

A: No, not really. In fact, with Dan and that other boy, they were kinda rivals and didn't bond at all. Maybe it was because people confused them, and I think it was insulting to Dan.

Sara raises an important point here concerning her brother's "rivalry" with the other Asian-American male. Since few Asians attended their school, it is telling that both found themselves being mistaken for other Asian-American children. Rather than feeling camaraderie for the other boy on the basis of being Asian in a predominantly white setting, Sara's brother felt pitted against him and therefore resentful of his presence. He subsequently distanced himself from the boy in the hopes of eliminating the possibility of being mistaken for him. This was yet another strategy some respondents adopted in trying to fit into their predominantly white neighborhood.

The theme of dissociating from other Asians as well as one's own Asianness in the hopes of being seen as an individual came up a number of times. For example, when asked whether she sought out other Asian-American children in school, Beth Chang, a third-generation Chinese-American in her late forties, replied: "I was one of only five Asians who went to my school but, no, we kinda avoided each other because we didn't want to seem cliquish . . . [but] we saw each other because it was easy to spot. We waved but we never really became good friends." Being perceived as "cliquish" struck a nerve for many. Through further probing, it became clear that this term along with other descriptive labels such as conforming, nerdy, too "straight," and overly academic were seen as embodying popular Asian stereotypes and were to be avoided if possible.

Asian immigrants, in particular, were lightning rods for resentment and avoidance since they were seen as fueling stereotypes and giving "all Asians a bad name." Jerry Fong reflected on his actions at an earlier stage in his life:

In high school I avoided them in a way. I think in my high school the majority of the Asians were nerds. . . . It's just the fact that they were fobs in a way. They were like F.O.B.s, and I was better than them because I was more assimilated, and I had more friends, and I could go to the local burger stand and not be laughed at because I dressed the same as the rest of the kids did, and I basically talked the same. And so because they talked different, they were foreign. It basically came out to they were foreign. I didn't purposely seek them out, in a way I kinda avoided them, not in a sense of not knowing them because I knew them because I was involved in school activities and stuff. And so I knew them, but beyond knowing them, as far as calling them up and saying, "Hey, let's go out," or something, I wouldn't do that.

The dilemma that Jerry and others faced centered around the importance they placed on the opinions of their white peers. The presence of "fobs," a derogatory term standing for "fresh off the boat," complicated Jerry's status in his community because the chances of being mistaken for one were high in his mind. This led to his need to dissociate from them and, more important, to prove to himself that he was not like them. Reflecting years later on the situation, Jerry spoke remorsefully about his actions: "I didn't want to be seen outside of school, outside of the educational environment with these fobs. It's so freakin' terrible." In other words, the price Jerry paid for living in a racist and nativist society involved closing himself off from getting to know or befriend Asian immigrants.

Really what was at issue for respondents similar to Jerry was their apprehension of losing their sense of individuality in the face of crude stereotypes, a finding that corroborates Osajima's (1993) work: "The desire to distance themselves from the stereotypical Asian image constitutes another hidden injury, a sense of discomfort around and disgust toward other Asians" (p. 86). By dissociating not only from immigrants but other Asian-Americans, they hoped could be seen as individuals and not as racial and/or ethnic types. As we have seen, however, this strategy was far from foolproof.

Finally, Rick Wubara, a Yonsei in his late twenties, described how he deflected attention away from his Asianness in order to fit in when his family moved to Walnut Creek, a white bedroom community in northern California:

Q: Did you experience any prejudice directed at you as an Asian?

A: Well, yeah. Just more like ignorance, people just ignorantly saying things like you know, chinaman or whatever. Things like that. Things I can ignore. I just don't take it seriously because I don't know the person or whatever. . . . Well, thinking about when I was growing up I always felt like I was just as good at whatever I did. Like basketball or school. So I think if I wasn't as good as they were, then maybe I would have had a little more prejudice against me. But because I was able to hang, they didn't see me so much as being Asian, or inferior because I was Asian. They just saw me as, "Oh well, I'll take him on my team." Because back then I don't think they're developed enough to really think those things out. But for me personally, I think the way I stayed away from it, it's not that I didn't think about it, I mean I always thought about it but [pause] but I made sure that it never had to come up because I kind of did my best to divert their attention away from me being Asian and just have them see me as being [pause] good [pause] or acceptable. I guess in a way it's like assimilating. I don't think I consciously did it back then, but when I look back, that's what I did. That's what I do now still.

At the beginning of the passage, Rick denied any emotional charge from the incidents that occurred, claiming he ignored such acts or attributed them to ignorance. But as he progressed with the story, Rick, far from ignoring them, paid an inordinate amount of attention to these acts and invested serious thought into ways of avoiding such situations; by the end he had completely contradicted himself by acknowledging that he "always thought about it." This passage aptly illustrates the process of self-deception and denial that often takes place to protect our self-esteem. Furthermore, it is telling that Rick chose to label his behavior as "assimilating" since the strategy he chose to follow hinged on his success at nullifying his Asian roots in the eyes of his white peers.

I would like to reflect for a moment longer on this passage because it illustrates so well the subtle and progressively corrosive wound inflicted by the "hidden injuries" of racial marginalization. In the case of intentional prejudice, the accompanying reaction is typically immediate and intense; hostility is detected and an involuntary response (anger, fear, shame, etc.) is felt. With racial marginalization, the effect is incremental, slowly chipping away at one's self-concept. Rationalizations are offered and incidents shrugged off in order to protect one's self-esteem. But all the while a running tab is kept on these cumulative "acts of ignorance," and increasingly the person spends more mental and emotional energy to short-circuit future incidents. Deflecting attention away from one's Asianness, avoiding associating with, and otherwise looking down upon other Asian-Americans, all reflect a steep price paid to overcome alienation. The irony, however, as Rick's confession reveals, is that peace of mind remains elusive; even after doing all of this, he remained vigilant and active in his efforts to gain social acceptance.

"It was more a gradual thing than all at once, but it felt comfortable": The Strategy of Seeking Out Other Asian-Americans

Not all sought to distance themselves from the few other Asians attending their school. A third strategy adopted, particularly by women, involved seeking out others either in classes or school clubs. Meg Takahashi,

> I went to basically a Caucasian school where I was like sometimes the only Oriental in class, period.
>
> Q: Did you seek out Asian-Americans?
> A: Yeah, because I was highly encouraged to by my mother. I mean [pause] she still accepted Caucasian friends, but any other race was discouraged.

Those who sought out other Asian-Americans did so because they believed they shared something in common with them. These included: similar upbringing, values, goals, and even experiences with racial marginalization. Parents, too, played a role in fostering these friendships, as Meg's account demonstrates. It is important to note, however, that Meg did not extend her invitation for friendship to nonassimilated Asians. Rather, she and others sought out Asians like themselves, ones who were Americanized.

A corollary to the third strategy involved associating with other Asian-Americans through extracurricular activities outside their neighborhood and school. About a fourth of our respondents who lived in white communities cultivated friendships with coethnics or other Asians by attending a language school, participating in Asian youth and sports leagues on the weekends, or attending ethnic church services and youth groups. Bill Saito's experience was typical. Even after moving to Agoura Hills, his parents continued to return to West Los Angeles on the weekends so he could play sports for a Japanese-American youth league while they visited with friends/kin, shopped, or ran errands. Another example, Patti Ito, a Yonsei in her mid-twenties, grew up in Anaheim when there were few Asian-Americans. Yet, she described her childhood circle of friends as including other Japanese ethnics similar to herself, that is, other young Japanese-American teens living in white neighborhoods. Patti befriended them through a Japanese-American sports league and youth group:

> The people I met who were Japanese hung out with all white people during the week too. And I think they kind of thought our friendship was special because we were Japanese and we finally met other people who were Japanese too.

The impetus for going beyond their neighborhoods to meet other Asians came not from respondents, but rather from their parents who felt for them to socialize with young people like themselves was important. As Rick Wubara described: "I think they sensed that that was the only place where I was going to meet any Asian people." Patti's mother, Lorraine Ito, reflected on why she enrolled her daughter and son in ethnic youth and sports leagues:

> [A]nd then when they were older, they were not meeting any Japanese people. So right before my daughter was in junior high, I kept saying maybe you should join SEYO, which is the Japanese-American youth organization here in Orange County. But they didn't feel the need, so that's when my husband and I insisted that they have to meet Japanese kids. At that point, I think I was letting them decide for themselves, but because they were growing up in Caucasian areas like I did, and

because I felt closer to Japanese people after meeting them at an older age, I felt it was important for them to meet Japanese people too. . . . However, I don't think I ever made them feel that they could not have Caucasian friends. They were welcome in the home or go out with them. Especially my son, when he usually dated the Caucasian people for the school dances. I don't think I ever made the girls feel unwelcome. And I don't think I ever made my son feel that he could not take out a Caucasian person or a Mexican person.

Lorraine felt it was important for her children to meet other Japanese kids because she remembered her own experiences growing up in a white community and the alienation she had sometimes experienced. Being around other Japanese ethnics felt comfortable to her, and she wanted to give her children the opportunity to develop similar relationships. Since there was a slim chance for meeting other Japanese ethnics in their own community, she took it upon herself to place them where they would. As an aside, Lorraine's children today associate primarily with other Japanese-Americans as well as Asian-Americans.

While some organizations offered traditional cultural lessons, most young people participated in such all-American pastimes as basketball, baseball/softball, and Christian Sunday school.[2] In short, the ethnic aspect to these activities had to do primarily with the fellowship. Bershtel and Graubard (1993) and Nagel (1994) discuss similar patterns in their work on contemporary Jewish-Americans and Native-Americans, respectively. In summarizing the state of the Jewish mainstream, Bershtel and Graubard (1993) argue, "what is done under the label Jewish is hardly distinguishable from what other middle-class Americans do" (p. 109). For example, a sampling of the activities offered by a Jewish community center include: karate, a baby-sitting clinic, folk music, and macrame, activities that hardly epitomize Jewish culture in any traditional sense.

While the authors take a cynical view of these activities as illustrative of cultural decay, I agree with Nagel's (1994) assessment that, "[C]ultures change; they are borrowed, blended, rediscovered, and reinterpreted" (p. 162). Few would dispute that as minority groups have incorporated American cultural patterns into their cultural repertoire, the line between ethnic and mainstream activities has blurred. After all, as Gordon (1964) argues, these are *parallel* institutions offering the same activities as mainstream institutions. Not diminishing the significance of people's choices is important, however. Participants (or in this case their parents) choose to join *ethnic* sports leagues and clubs rather than general ones because they believe in the value of coethnic or panethnic association.

"It was a completely isolated Chinese community. We had no contact with Caucasians at all": Growing Up in an Asian-centered Neighborhood

Another third of our respondents grew up in neighborhoods where other Asian-Americans or coethnics dominated. Older respondents typically recalled growing up in ethnically specific communities, the Chinese or Japanese sections of town, and described these as enclaves unto themselves. As Peter Gong, who grew up in San Francisco's Chinatown in the late 1920s, recalled, "Almost no Chinese spoke English in those days." Audrey Mah, a retired school principal in her late sixties, also grew up in Chinatown, but a much smaller one:

> It's in the city, in Santa Barbara, in what we call Chinatown. Just one corner of Santa Barbara. I understand that they are going to tear the whole thing down. . . . I don't think there were more than 100 people. It was about two and a half blocks, on one side of the street. We had a grocery store on the corner, a laundry, a couple other stores, and a shop. Quite a few gambling houses. I recently met up with somebody who is going to write up on Santa Barbara Chinatown. She's been digging into the history. She has a map of Santa Barbara from the 1800s, and she has about six to eight gambling houses on the map. This is by the Census. They knew where the houses were. One was owned by my grandfather, or at least he had a lot to do with it.

In Audrey's case, her adolescent world consisted of literally a few blocks and only a hundred or so Chinese people; interactions with whites were largely limited to the classroom and school yard because of strict racial mores. Furthermore, because she grew up during the 1930s, her community was dominated by men, which was true of most Chinese-American enclaves until well into the twentieth century (Wong, 1995).

Younger respondents, in contrast, were equally likely to mention growing up in pan-Asian communities as ethnically specific ones. These demographic differences between younger and older respondents reflect large-scale changes that have taken place in recent years as revisions in immigration law have taken effect and social barriers between second-generation and later Asian ethnic groups have diminished (Espiritu, 1992; Min, 1995). As a result, younger respondents have grown up experiencing more diversity within their communities, both generational and panethnic, compared with older respondents.[3]

Younger respondents, in particular, grew up seeing other Asian-Americans in a variety of mainstream roles (teacher, council member, shopkeeper, doctor, bank teller) as well as in positions of power in local city governments and schools. Jan Muramoto, a Sansei in her late thirties, characterized growing up in Gardena:

> [A]nd I was lucky to be in the kind of community that I grew up in. We were the student body presidents of Gardena High School, we were the yearbook editors, and all that we did. Maybe not me personally, but my whole generation did that. We were the leaders of the school, and when my daughter goes and my son too, [they] will be the leaders too.

Like those who grew up in predominantly white neighborhoods, younger respondents such as Jan joined Boy/Girl Scouts and Brownies, went to McDonald's for burgers and fries, and celebrated the Fourth of July just like everybody else. What made their experience different was that the other kids in their troop were typically Asian-Americans, McDonald's may have been found in an Asian strip mall or next to an Asian-owned auto parts store, and along with traditional American holidays their community celebrated various ethnic festivals as well (for example, Nisei Week, Chinese New Year's, Cherry Blossom Festival, Moon Festival). So while their communities clearly offered all of the trappings of a typical American neighborhood, they also had a distinct ethnic flavor to them.

Most of the Asian-centered communities described to us were in California, which was not surprising since more Asians are concentrated there than anywhere else in the nation (Barringer et al., 1993). Frequently mentioned communities included Gardena, Torrance, West Los Angeles, San Gabriel, Monterey Park, San Marino, Daly City, San Francisco's Sunset District and Chinatown, and Oakland's China Hill. In some cases the communities they mentioned were the same ones their own parents had grown up in, which usually meant that extended kin (uncles, aunts, grandparents, cousins) also lived in the area.

Outside California, Asian-centered communities that were mentioned were found in Hawaii. About a fourth of our respondents who grew up in predominantly Asian communities were raised or spent the early part of their adolescence on one of the islands, reflecting the closely knit ties linking the two states; historically, many Asian-Americans made their way to California after having first established themselves in Hawaii (Takaki, 1989b). Japanese-Americans, in particular, have deep roots in Hawaii because of their heavy recruitment earlier in the century to work the sugarcane fields and cultivate plantation lands; six out of the eight respondents born in Hawaii are of Japanese descent.

Not surprisingly, our respondents recalled having many Asian-Americans in their adolescent social cliques, friendships formed at school as well as in the neighborhood. There was no need to make a conscious effort to seek out Asian friends because of their ready availability—"they were what was around." Instead, friendships with whites took effort since few lived in the community; some respondents would wait until college to have their first sustained interactions with whites. Also mentioned were memberships in the same ethnic organizations that respondents who grew up in white communities had to commute to in to order to participate. A few downplayed joining ethnic organizations, however, citing their own uninterest or the lack of insistence on their parents' part—living in Asian-centered communities provided their children with enough exposure to other Asian-Americans and to their culture.

When asked to reflect on their awareness of being Chinese, Japanese, or Asian-American during adolescence, most claimed it was a nonissue since everyone else around them was of similar ancestry. Blauner's (1972) discussion of the racial privilege usually accorded whites in American society is useful here since the privilege he refers to is based on the freedom of not having to think about one's racial background. It is the privilege to be considered "normal," to have one's race be irrelevant. Respondents who grew up in Asian-centered communities possessed, to varying degrees, racial privilege *within the context of their neighborhood*. Frank Wu, a fifth-generation Chinese-American who grew up in San Francisco's Chinatown in the late 1940s and early 1950s, had this to say:

Q: How conscious were you of being Chinese?

A: If you lived in San Francisco Chinatown, you are completely absorbed in the culture as well as language. So in that sense it was normal. I don't know if you were really conscious of it. I guess my parents' family and ourselves, we were pretty proud of the fact that we were Chinese and Americans at the same time. My parents' generation was an unusually balanced generation. They lived in the ghetto and never really left it, but at the same time were very very Americanized. Perfectly fluent English. . . . But at the same time we all preferred to live in the Chinese culture and pursue it, and the Chinese customs and the food of course, and our friends were predominantly Chinese.

Frank's comment, "it was normal," captures the defining element of racial privilege—as a child he had the privilege to be seen as normal because everyone else around him was also Chinese. Within the confines of his community, he wasted no energy thinking about his Chineseness or how others evaluated it.

Besides Frank's observation of the normality of being Chinese, I was struck by how proudly he emphasized his family's dual mastery of both Chinese and American culture. Except for a few older respondents who grew up isolated, some, when asked to reflect on their awareness of being Chinese, Japanese, or Asian, reiterated Frank's comments. While proud of their ancestry, they repeatedly stressed how acculturated they were. Lonnie Wong, a third-generation Chinese-American in her twenties, described her experiences growing up in San Francisco's Chinatown and Sunset District:

> A lot of my friends are the same generation as I. We all spoke English. I don't think anybody spoke Chinese that we hung around with. It wasn't a big problem, I didn't even think about it back then. Oh, I went to Chinese school and stuff, the regular deal for a few years, but of course I don't remember anything, and you don't really learn too much. Just kinda day-care thing. I was six or seven.

While not explicitly expressed by all, one of the reasons for stressing their cultural savviness had to do with their insistence on distinguishing themselves from Asian immigrants. They were defensive about their generational status and wished to make clear the ways they differed from the immigrants; they were American-ized, completely fluent in English, contributed to their community, and were not "pushy" or aggressive. Just because they were raised in Asian-centered communities then, did not mean they were im-mune to the intolerance respondents raised in white communities felt toward Asian immigrants. Immigrants "pushed their buttons" just as they did for those raised in white communities and for simi-lar reasons.

While inadvertent prejudice was rare because of the unique dynamics in their neighborhoods, incidents of intentional preju-dice were still common. More than half recalled experiencing ra-cially charged episodes during their adolescence. Such incidents typically took place outside their communities, for example, dur-ing family vacations or at a shopping mall in a nearby city. Some were specific to older respondents such as tensions with non-Asians living in neighboring boroughs. Peter Gong recalled the skirmishes that occasionally broke out between Chinese and Italians in 1920s San Francisco:

> *Q:* Did you ever encounter any racism or discrimination as a kid?
> *A:* Oh, we did have our share of it in San Francisco. The people in North Beach, they'd throw rocks at us. But their parents taught them, so they did what their parents taught them. They weren't in groups or gangs, it was the individual.

Q: How did your parents react?

A: Oh, I wouldn't tell them. I'd get a beating. I'd be accused of provoking them. It was so ingrained in us that we lay low and kept our distance from any activity that would expose us to any competition. We were not militant, we were militant inside, but we couldn't express it. My father was a very strong, dictatorial, chauvinistic father, like all Chinese fathers were. You never talked back, you never said no. I got my share of heavy beatings. I did learn. Anyways, things do change.

Furthermore, only older respondents mentioned experiencing racial segregation in school. Audrey Mah, for example, described how minority students were tracked into classes different from those that wealthier white students in Santa Barbara attended:

> Then when we got to high school [pause] there were only two junior high schools in Santa Barbara. One was all white, upper-class white. So when we met in high school, we knew who was who, because they separated us. Most of us were separated. The whites in one class, the mixed in another class.

Older respondents were also subject to xenophobic fears and racism surrounding World War II. It is well known that Japanese ethnics experienced severe discrimination during the war that culminated in their internment. Older Chinese ethnics, however, also recalled suffering from nativist fears during the war. Shirley Hum, a third-generation Chinese-American in her sixties, recalled the special badge she was told to wear during the war: "I just remember when the Japanese were taken to the camps, we would all wear badges saying we were Chinese-Americans. That kind of thing, so we would not be mistaken."

Respondents raised in Asian-centered communities, like those raised in white communities, also could not avoid moments of insecurity and self-criticism over their appearance and how it differed from mainstream (read: white) images they saw in film, television, and magazines. Like other teenagers growing up in the 1970s, Jan Muramoto was swept up in the Farrah Fawcett "wavy and feathered hair" craze popularized by the TV show *Charlie's Angels*:

I think in high school you grow up with a lot of the girls who are bleaching out their hair, and stuff. There was that age, you'll die, without that Farrah Fawcett hairdo. And I went in and said I want my hair like that, and the hairdresser said, "Janice, you're Japanese. You have straight, strong, pokey hair. I cannot make it look like that." And you get this sudden revelation like, oh, okay. I should be proud of the hair I have. It's straight. It's strong and that's just the way it is. And I go through this with my daughter. This is our hair, our eyes. You should be proud of it.

Jan experienced a crucial revelation by acknowledging not only that she was physically different from the mainstream white women she saw on television but in accepting this fact without any sense of shame. The importance of the latter part, the lack of shame, cannot be stressed enough since so many of our respondents who felt racially alienated as children did experience shame. Jan successfully reinterpreted her physical differences as positive features of her identity, and I suspect this was helped by the availability of positive role models in her community who were also Asian-American.

"It was a relatively diverse suburb [with] a good mix of Caucasians, African Americans, Latin Americans, some Asian Americans": Growing Up in a Racially Diverse Neighborhood

The remainder of our respondents grew up in communities where some combination of whites, blacks, Asians, and/or Hispanics resided. Commonly mentioned places included: Oakland, Berkeley, Daly City, Santa Monica, Venice, Silverlake, and Griffith Park. Some who lived in Monterey Park before the recent and heavy influx of Chinese immigrants mentioned that city.

Unlike respondents who were raised in predominantly white or Asian communities, no clear patterns of racial alienation or comfort, or of inadvertent or intentional prejudice emerged. Rather, experiences varied depending upon the particular history of the community and local dynamics. Some recalled race and ethnicity as highly permeable boundaries while others had a completely different experience where racial and ethnic distinctions were clearly drawn. Susan Mineta thought the mix in her neighborhood, Gardena in the late 1940s, was ideal: "At the time I'd say mostly white, and then the next biggest group would probably be Asian, Japanese. Not too many Chinese, some black, some Mexican. I think it was a real nice balance." Eileen Inouye, in contrast, recalled simmering tensions in her community as groups clashed over class, racial, and generational differences:

> Our elementary school was really nice, and then we were just sort of tossed into this junior high that was in another city even. Mostly Hispanic. And they resented us. I guess it was sort of bad because we grew up in a middle- to upper-middle-class neighborhood, and the Hispanic kids were coming from very poor areas. And you mix them up, and you know they really resented the fact that we were even there. . . . I think that really shaped my impressions or how I felt about Hispanic people. I guess because they didn't accept us, we were very reluctant to accept them at the same time. So it was pretty bad. . . . Growing up I thought, gosh, Hispanic people are awful. They don't like us. They kick in our locker doors.

Eileen described the resentment Hispanic students felt at being encroached upon by students like herself who were non-Hispanic and middle class. Later in the interview, however, she described another group targeted for resentment, in this case wealthy Chinese immigrants who were seen as "taking over" the community and schools:

Q: Did things change when you went to high school?

A: No, they got even worse because now the Hispanic kids were pretty much judging us based on what we looked like. And during that time in Monterey Park, there was a big influx of Chinese immigrants which, they practically took over Monterey Park. And that was a big resentment. I think as Japanese-Americans we resented that also because they just took over the city council and rezoned a lot of the residential districts to house condos. And it really made it a crowded city, and a lot of people resented that. Too much growth in such a short amount of time because within five years the whole city just turned upside down. And that was one thing I remember, really resenting the Chinese people as well as the Hispanic people. So it really left a small minority of Japanese-Americans that had to stick together.

Q: And how did the Caucasians fit in?

A: There was a big white flight out of Monterey Park at that time. So a lot of our Caucasian friends just left.

I was struck by the irony captured in Eileen's description of what took place in her community. The resentment she and other Japanese ethnics directed at Chinese immigrants was not very different from the resentment Hispanics targeted at her own group earlier; one group was seen as encroaching upon the territory of another. Yet she did not recognize the link between the Chinese and Japanese students because ethnic and generational differences stood out more strongly in her mind (Hayano, 1981; Saito, 1993). Compounding her resentment, after all, was that non-Asians failed to differentiate between Japanese ethnics like herself and the recently arrived Chinese[4]—"the Hispanic kids were pretty much judging us based on what we looked like." As discussed in earlier sections of this chapter, to be mistaken for an immigrant was anathema to respondents who lived in white as well as Asian communities. The same applied to respondents who grew up in diverse communities.

In general, their friendship circles reflected the diversity available in the community, although about a quarter conceded their circle was top heavy with Asian-Americans. Only a handful attributed this to dynamics similar to those described by Eileen; the rest described how their circle formed as a matter of coincidence and shared interests. Jenny Kato, a Sansei in her twenties, had this to say:

Q: Who were your closest friends in school?

A: Asians and Caucasians.

Q: Did you purposely seek out other Asians, or did it just turn out that way?

A: I think it just turned out that way, at least in elementary school.
Well [pause] junior high [pause] well, I would still have been open,
but I guess I started changing, hanging around with more Asians;
I think more because those were the people in my classes. By junior high you start getting into honors classes, and there just tended
to be a lot of Asians there that had similar backgrounds and interests like clubs, whatever. So that's just what happened. So it
wasn't purposely like wanting to just hang out with Asians.

Once a friendship started, other factors encouraged its development. Some parents, for instance, encouraged their children to
develop friendships with other Asians. Shared academic and extracurricular interests were also mentioned. After seeing the same
faces in the same classes, friendships naturally developed as students formed study groups and worked on assignments together.
Karen Murakami described how her circle of friends changed from
predominantly white to Asian:

> When I got to Marshall, I really didn't know a lot of people be-
> cause a lot of my girlfriends still went to the Catholic school. When
> I got to high school, all the people in my classes, honors classes,
> were Asian, and I ended up being friends with them. I guess at
> that time I started to feel more comfortable with those people.
> Q: What do you mean, comfortable?
> A: Well, they were in the same classes with me, had the same goals.
> Q: Do you think you sought out Asian friends in high school?
> A: Yeah, in a way. I was in a new school, didn't really know a lot of
> people. These people in the classes, maybe they looked like me
> [laugh] or something. Made me feel more comfortable.

Meeting other Asians through weekend activities such as ethnic churches and sports leagues came up as well. Gary Hong, a
fourth-generation Chinese-American in his early twenties, described his involvement with a sports league:

> I played on these Japanese/Asian-American sports leagues in the
> Bay Area, for baseball and basketball. I played in those since sec-
> ond, third grade. I didn't do the conventional little leagues. I
> played in these Asian leagues. That provides you with a network

of people, Asian-American families, kids and parents in the East Bay. That was during the week too. Families would do things, so I had contact everywhere.

Q: Why Japanese/Asian leagues instead of conventional ones?

A: Because my parents [pause] it goes throughout the entire East Bay. My dad, when he was growing up he knew a lot of guys who were Asian-American, most of them reside in Berkeley still. When your kids are growing up, they talk about, "Oh yeah, my son's playing this league." The leagues been around a long time and sorta like the generational thing: "I played, my son is gonna play in this." My Dad knew people, he didn't play in it but knew people whose sons were playing in it. They said, "Yeah, have your son come out." So I went and signed up.

Similar to Asian ethnics who grew up in white neighborhoods, these ethnic outlets provided them with a ready network of Asian-Americans to befriend. The pattern of interaction that emerged—diverse friends during the weekdays, followed by Asian friends on the weekends—characterized approximately one fourth of the friendship circles of our respondents.

In Eileen Inouye's case, awareness of being Japanese ran very high because of the dynamics in her community—"So it really left a small minority of Japanese-Americans who had to stick together." Moreover, it was specifically a Japanese-American rather than Asian-American awareness she felt since she clearly distinguished herself from the Chinese immigrants in her community. Fred Yang, in contrast, spoke of only a passing awareness of being Chinese. A third-generation Chinese-American who grew up in Berkeley in the 1950s, Fred discussed the irrelevance of racial and ethnic labels in his community: "[T]he thing was I grew up in such an integrated neighborhood it wasn't a big deal to be Chinese or black or something like that."

Some recalled developing an early consciousness based on regular visits to nearby ethnic communities. Chinese respondents who grew up in the Bay Area, for example, described how they frequently went to San Francisco's Chinatown to visit kin and shop for ethnic food and goods. Gary Hong's experience provides a good illustration:

I was very conscious [of being Chinese], especially given the fact that I had so much contact with Chinatown, the weekend trips, the interactions with the sports teams and people at school. I just didn't think about it too much. I knew they were Chinese and Asian-American also, but we were doing things very American, the American aspect of the Asian-American label but with Asian people. . . . I knew that Asian people could do American things but still be among Asian.

Once again, the theme of pride in ancestry alongside an emphasis on being American comes through. Gary was indeed conscious of being Chinese, and yet it was not something he fixated on. He had sustained interactions with other Chinese and Asians, both within his community and beyond, but was aware that these friendships were not ethnically focused.

▧ *Summary*

Through their interactions with friends and strangers outside the home, our respondents learned the importance others placed on their racial and ethnic identities. For those who grew up in predominantly white communities, their racial rather than ethnic identity was salient. All were made aware to varying degrees of being racially "different" and were reminded in both inadvertent and meanspirited forms. Both carried a sting although inadvertent prejudice may have taken a greater toll in the long run because of the gradual but cumulative effect it had on their sense of self-esteem.

Respondents raised in Asian-centered communities enjoyed the greatest degree of freedom from thinking of themselves in racial or ethnic terms. They expended much less energy thinking about how others perceived them because they had the luxury of racial privilege, of being "normal," within the context of their community.

No clear patterns emerged among respondents raised in racially diverse communities. For some, race and ethnicity were clearly salient aspects of their identity (along with generational status and social class) because of their significance to the wider community. These components of their identities were salient wherever tensions along racial and ethnic lines existed. Conversely, for respondents raised in communities relatively free from tension, middling salience was assigned to their racial and ethnic identities; they spoke of the free and easy interactions they often experienced across racial and ethnic lines.

"Practicality ◻ CHAPTER 5 always steps in"
The Continuing Erosion of Cultural Traditions in Adulthood

Many years have passed since our respondents first learned the significance (or lack thereof) of traditional Chinese or Japanese culture for their families. Now as adults, many with their own families, they are deciding for themselves what part, if any, ethnicity should play in their lives. Considering what they have already said about their childhoods, to learn that most do not lead what would traditionally be defined as ethnically embedded lifestyles should come as no surprise. They were not raised to do so as children, and it would have been unlikely for them to do so as adults.

Similar to white ethnics, they exercise a great deal of personal choice regarding the traditional cultural elements they wish to keep or discard (Alba, 1990; Crispino, 1980; Gans, 1979; Kellogg, 1990; Waters, 1990). By commonly accepted indicators, the majority have chosen to retain very little. Most cannot speak Chinese or Japanese save a few scattered words, do not celebrate ethnic holidays with fanfare or reverence, have not meaningfully or consistently incorporated traditional customs into their lifestyles, are increasingly likely to date and marry outside their ethnic group, and are not particularly concerned with raising their children to carry on cultural traditions.

"I can speak food. That's about it":
Ethnic Language Use

Although a third of our respondents attended language school anywhere from a few weeks to a few years during adolescence; rare was the individual who retained very much from those early lessons. Now as adults, most consider English the only language they speak. Similar to their white ethnic counterparts, they are continuing the shift away from ethnic language use toward a total reliance on English (Alba, 1990; Veltman, 1983). At best, some joked they could "speak food" or recall simple words and phrases but nothing that added up to a comprehensive vocabulary.

One reason language retention is poor centers around the lack of opportunities to speak regularly. The absolute dominance of the English language in both public and private life actively discourages bilingualism (Alba & Nee, 1996; Gans, 1979). Even respondents such as Lonnie Wong, who went to Chinese school as a child and today wishes she were fluent, acknowledged the impracticality of her desire:

> I wish I knew Chinese. I wouldn't say that specifically makes me Chinese, that that is the element that you need to be Chinese, but personally I would like to so I could communicate more with the other generations. . . . I would think, man, if I learn Chinese I would make my kids learn Chinese. [But] I don't think that's realistic because I don't think I'd be talking Chinese a lot anyways. To tell you the truth, if I knew Chinese I wouldn't know where I'd be using it except if I had a job where speaking Chinese was a necessity.

Lonnie perceptively recognized that if she were fluent today, the opportunities to speak Chinese would be limited. Instead of integrating the knowledge into her daily life, she would likely compartmentalize and use Chinese only occasionally. Even with her coethnic friends, she does not speak Chinese except the occasional phrase or word dropped here or there. Tellingly, Lonnie also admitted that even if her (future) children were to learn Chinese, she probably would not speak regularly with them. Her longing to speak Chinese is based more on a romantic notion of what the language symbolizes and a wistful urge to be closer to her ethnic heritage than a realistic desire to incorporate it into her lifestyle. Hansen (1938) noted the same tendency among third-generation white ethnics that he attributed to their nostalgic longing to reclaim the culture of their immigrant grandparents.

Others acknowledged the inevitable shift toward English monolingualism and spoke of the futility of fighting against this aspect of acculturation. Carol Wong, a dietician in her fifties, was raised understanding that English would be her primary language:

> My dad, his method was, you're Chinese, so you're good. You don't have to worry any further. That was his attitude. He said, but you're in this country. You're never going to live in China unless something horrendous happens. He says, you know that the culture you come from is good, you know a little bit about the food. He says, you know something about the country, the history. . . . He said, but I've seen so many people who hang onto the language. They hang on and they force their kids to do things they don't wanna do, and a few generations after, you know, there's a lot of headache for something that is going to happen, regardless. If your children, your grandchildren, your great-grandchildren are going to be in this country, they're gonna learn that language, and they're going to want to know the customs.

Carol's father was a pragmatic man. In his mind, language loss was unavoidable, a simple fact and cost of immigration. Therefore, over time it was better not to fight against the inevitable and to be proud of your heritage—to know that because "you're Chinese, you're good." Carol accepted her father's philosophy and has carried it on in her own life; she has not raised her fourth-generation sons to speak Chinese.

Morrison Hum, a retired school principal, also chose not to raise his fourth-generation son to speak Chinese:

> A: My son married a Chinese from up in the [San Francisco] Bay Area.

Q: But your son doesn't particularly teach his children much about Chinese culture?

A: No, uh uh. . . . We never really passed it on to him, the language or the culture. Just the holidays maybe, Chinese New Year's. That's it.

Q: Is there a reason why you didn't pass it on?

A: Well, because there are no [pause] because the language too, you are learning English and speaking English. . . . Then you are living in a white world. You figure that it's not that important because you are mingling with white people when you are growing up and the school system is white and all that, so you don't.

Here Morrison brings up the important issue of social risk. He believed that learning Chinese would have been inappropriate for his son because he lives "in a white world" where English so clearly dominates. Without explicitly stating so, the underlying tone in Morrison's comments expresses his concern about drawing unwanted attention to his son. As a racial minority, his son already ran the risk of encountering racism; speaking Chinese might have compounded the situation by leaving him open to nativistic accusations of being a foreigner and unpatriotic.

Nor are Morrison's concerns particularly irrational or paranoid. Language, one of the most obvious symbols of cultural difference, has historically been an easy target for nativist resentment (Takaki, 1993b). Retaining one's ethnic language was tantamount to rejecting assimilationist principles and therefore an affront to nativists' demands for cultural and linguistic conformity. Racialized ethnics who held onto their language were subject to double jeopardy since they triggered both racist and nativist anxieties.

Today, linguistic diversity remains a hot-button issue, especially in states such as California that have recently experienced exponential growth among their non–English-speaking population. That these populations also happen to be seen as racially different has only added to the sense of threat experienced by sectors of the white population who feel they are being "taken over" (Pimentel, 1995; U.S. Commission on Civil Rights, 1986). Sensing this, some of our respondents and their parents decided to take the path of quick acculturation, hoping this action would reduce chances for dissonance. Such a strategy informed Morrison's decision regarding his son.

In short, there are social risks involved that Asian ethnics must weigh when deciding whether to retain or relearn their ethnic language. These risks are tied into the assumption of foreignness that hovers over them despite their generational longevity.

▒ *"It just depends on who I'm around": Ethnic Holidays and Events*

A general fickleness characterizes our respondents' attitudes toward celebrating ethnic holidays. Carl Ito captured this sentiment best by acknowledging his family celebrates "when we remember," a statement that speaks directly to the increasingly voluntary and casual nature of ritual observance for Asian ethnics. Today, there is even less of a sense of obligation to observing ethnic holidays than during their childhoods. At best, some expressed mild guilt over their lax behavior and spoke about doing better in the future. These declarations, although sincere, should be viewed with some skepticism, however. Without proximate family members or a salient ethnic community to keep ethnic holidays embedded within meaningful social networks, observance is entirely dependent on self-motivation. Naturally, this usually does not go very far. Carl, for example, expressed a heartfelt belief in the value of celebrating ethnic holidays so his young children would be in touch with their heritage and "know where they come from." But he and his Filipino-American wife have not consistently followed through on their good intentions as his earlier remark attests. Celebrating Filipino or Japanese holidays are sporadic events that they may or may not observe from year to year.

The importance of meaningful social networks in promoting communal participation should not be understated. In the past those ties functioned to anchor individuals to their ethnic community and otherwise ensure ritual observance (Yancey et al., 1976). As individuals have moved away from ethnically concentrated communities and into ethnically and racially diverse ones, holiday observance has become vulnerable to being discarded.

The passing away of elderly kin has further contributed to this vulnerability by removing yet another supportive "leg" to ritual observance. Jeremy Shih, a retired chemist, reflected on the effect his parents' deaths had on observance within his family:

> Since my father passed away [in] 1952 and my mother passed away [in] 1972 [pause] after they passed away we kind of forgot some of the Chinese customs. But some of my older brothers still have the Chinese customs. So on Chinese New Year they'll have a special Chinese dinner. But we used to pass out laycee. Now I think we've kind of forgotten some of these customs.

Without his parents to unite the family around ethnic holidays, Jeremy has drifted away from observing them. Of course, he did not raise his own children to observe either.

Fred Yang, a computer specialist in his late forties, also acknowledged his reliance on those around him for cultural inspiration:

Q: Do you celebrate any Chinese holidays?

A: No, I don't really. Chinese New Year, I don't know. It's just something that comes up but not something that I'm conscious of. It's not something that I purposely celebrate. I think it just depends on who I'm around. If I'm really in an Asian community [then] I'm aware of it.

It is understandable why celebrating Chinese New Year's is not at the forefront of Fred's thoughts and why he is likely to treat it as any other day unless others motivate him to celebrate. He has created a lifestyle that is simply not conducive to remembering. He lives in a white suburb in southern California where Chinese holidays hold little significance with his neighbors or community. Furthermore, his wife is not Chinese, and they do not have any children. Meanwhile, his parents live hundreds of miles away; moreover, he does not consider himself close to his family. Lastly, he has limited interactions with other Chinese-Americans both at work and when he plays. In short, his life is largely devoid of meaningful ethnic ties. Nobody is there to remind or chastise him if he forgets a holiday or chooses not to celebrate.

Those who currently live in Asian-centered communities, in

contrast to respondents such as Fred Yang, are more likely to celebrate at some level because of the structural supports in their communities that reinforce ethnic observance. It is difficult to ignore or forget holidays if one's network of neighbors and friends anticipate ethnic holidays and generate energy around celebrating. Someone is bound to be a motivating force to organize a get-together or chastize those who would rather not bother to celebrate. Similarly, flyers and banners posted in local supermarkets and stores announcing upcoming events in honor of the Chinese New Year, the Moon Festival, or the Obon Festival help to remind those who might not otherwise remember or know on what days these events fall.

Since most of our respondents do not live in Asian-centered communities, few have these structural supports to rely upon. Especially for those who are single and childless, they are simply not interested at this stage in their lives to put much energy into celebrations unless they are organized by other family members or friends. Many have simply stopped celebrating or else do so in what they feel are clearly superficial terms:

> I mean, if going out to dinner and getting money is celebration [laugh], I guess I do [celebrate Chinese New Year's].

> If you go to a Chinese New Year dance, is that celebrating?

Those with young children are more willing to place effort into exposing them to different holidays and festivals just as their parents did for them. And so they will take their children to see the activities surrounding Nisei Week or to see the Lion Parade during the Chinese New Year. But as often happened in their own upbringing, the emphasis is on exposure rather than forcing or expecting them to incorporate traditions into their lives. If the interest level of our respondents who were given the same choices when they were young is any indication, the likelihood of their children choosing to continue celebrating when they become adults is not very high.

▨ *"Practicality always steps in": The Erosion of Traditional Customs and Practices*

When asked to reflect on the personal importance of retaining cultural traditions and values in their lives, three distinct responses emerged. The first comes from those who believe it is important and expend energy to attend cultural events regularly, visit China or Japan, join historical and cultural organizations, or take classes in traditional Chinese or Japanese music, dance, and other fine arts. They are a small group, consisting mostly of older respondents who often are retired and have the time and resources to pursue these interests.

Those in the second group, the largest of the three, claim that culture is important but are at a loss to show how this is so in their lives. A marked disparity between their professed beliefs and actual practices characterizes this group. Peter Gong captures this sentiment in the following passage:

Q: How important is it for you to incorporate Chinese culture into your life?

A: More important than ever. . . .

Q: What do you do?

A: Well we don't observe with any ceremony. We are just more conscious of that. It isn't primary in our daily living, but wherever we can get a glimpse of it we will, we'll try. There is a Bok-Hai festival in Marysville, we thought of going to it, but the timing was not right. We wanted to go last year too, but [pause]. Then there is the Moon Festival here, but we've never made that either. So it's just a consciousness in the back of our minds.

Q: Why are you conscious of it?

A: There is a kinship. We feel comfortable. It just gives you a sense of belonging to a heritage, and it is reinforced more by my wife than it is by me. My children are not interested.

It is hard to miss the temperamental quality surrounding Peter Gong's efforts to catch "glimpses" of Chinese culture. Unless the timing is just right, Peter is unlikely to follow through on his good intentions because there is no sense of obligation to participate (Gans, 1979). Instead, the few cultural activities he engages in are done intermittently, with an air of novelty, not reverence.

Ultimately, being "conscious" of one's ethnic background is more important than participating in events, maintaining cultural traditions, or consistently associating with coethnics.

Peter's comments are more ironic than they appear. Peter credits his (second) wife for pushing him to expand his knowledge about Chinese culture. His wife, however, is not Chinese; she is white. According to Peter, she is more Chinese than he since she is the driving force behind their efforts to incorporate Chinese culture into their lives!

Respondents such as Peter are eager to claim the benefits that come from a salient ethnic identity (e. g., sense of kinship and comfort), but are unwilling to put forth much effort to sustain ethnic connections, a finding that fits Gans's (1979) notion of symbolic ethnicity. They engage in the easiest and most superficial forms of ethnic identification, an affiliation based more on the personal meaningfulness and enjoyment of ethnic symbols than the actual integration of cultural traditions into their lives. Take Meg Takahashi, for instance. She enjoys claiming an ethnic identity because it allows her to feel unique in a social climate that currently celebrates multiculturalism and getting in touch with one's ethnic roots. But the key to her enjoyment centers around its not demanding much effort on her part:

> It's a toughie. I think [culture's] important. I think that's where my identity is, uniqueness, which I do appreciate. I think all Americans want to be unique in some way, and that's my thing about being unique without a lot of effort. At the same time, I don't want to be overtly Japanese because then when I assimilate into the American culture, I think of myself as American first and then Japanese second.

Those in the second group also have a difficult time identifying what are uniquely core elements of Chinese or Japanese values. Instead, they tend to describe values that most middle-class Americans hold as specifically Chinese or Japanese in origin, a practice white ethnics engage in as well (Waters, 1990). Rob Yamaguchi's experience is illustrative here:

> *Q:* Was it important to your family that you be familiar with traditional Japanese culture?

A: I think they thought it was very important *based on what they knew* and what their parents had passed on to them. I think they were interested in getting us involved in church and meeting other Japanese in church. They wanted us to learn some of the values.

Q: What values?

A: I guess just studying and working hard, trying to succeed because they never had a formal college education so they were pretty much trying to instill in me those things.

Q: Do you think that is particularly Japanese?

A: No. I think any parent would want their kid to do well.

Q: How did they express the things they wanted to pass down?

A: Most of the holiday type events they would try to have some Japanese influences like New Year's. But it was really minimal because they didn't speak Japanese in the house. So I think those traditional values were kinda lost, I think in their opinion also. Through generations it kinda diminishes more and more.

Rob expresses both clarity and confusion in this passage. In terms of emergent Japanese-American cultural values (although he does not refer to them as such), he was clear about the expectations placed on him. His parents encouraged him to attend a (Christian) church with a predominantly Japanese-American congregation and to associate with coethnics. In terms of traditional Japanese values, however, Rob was much less confident since his family placed less importance on developing this area. He eventually conceded that the values he described as Japanese were universally championed by parents of all ethnicities.

While respondents in the second group at least claim to hold cultural traditions in high regard, those in the third group place little to no importance on retaining Chinese or Japanese traditions. They feel as Andrew Lee does: "It's not that important at all. It hasn't been impressed on me. As I grow older, part of me kinda wishes I knew some things, but I hardly make the attempt to learn anything." Andrew is clear about the role of cultural traditions in his life. While he wouldn't mind learning more and even wishes he "knew some things," he is not willing to put in the effort to acquire this knowledge. As stressed in the previous chapter, the rich meaning behind cultural activities was not "impressed" upon respondents such as Andrew when they were young, and so today they hold little sentiment for these practices.

Andrew's fiancée, Elise Lim, on the other hand, would like to integrate some traditions into their life when they marry but acknowledged the obstacles to doing so:

> For me a certain level of [culture] is very important, but practicality always steps in. You always have to do more of the fast meal preparation. Chinese takes a lot longer. If you define Chinese as anything with rice or oyster sauce, sesame oil, we have that a lot. . . . For me, it's trying to, like, what little I do know, whatever little opportunities I know, to tell my nephew. Because my sister doesn't really know them. My nephew is four years old. About a year ago I mentioned to him he was Chinese and he just laughed and laughed! He said, "No I'm not!" I said, "Yeah, you are." He said, "Nooo." It was because he thought Chinese was food. It was as if I was calling him a carrot or a banana.

Between Andrew's indifference and Elise's own limited knowledge combined with her busy schedule, it is unlikely the two will realistically change their lifestyle to incorporate Chinese traditions. The effort needed to do so is simply more than this young couple is likely to afford.

"It's so hard to find someone that you really like that race isn't the issue": Dating and Marriage Patterns

Even in matters of the heart, ethnicity clearly plays less and less of a role. That forty-four of the forty-eight single men and women we interviewed have dated outside of their ethnic group speaks directly to ethnicity's waning influence in a fundamental area of life. And while not all will necessarily intermarry, the fact that so many have dated out of their ethnic group suggests that a sizable portion may also marry out.

Dating out is practiced most freely by the current generation of young and single Asian ethnics. While the absolute norm for those less than forty years of age, it was the exception for older respondents (most of whom are now married to coethnics). As Wilma Lew, a third-generation Chinese-American in her sixties, remarked: "It just wasn't done. . . . You're talking about forty years ago. You didn't do that. Now, it's more common. I never even thought about it." Compare Wilma's comments to Daphne Kitano's, a Yonsei in her mid-twenties:

> I don't really give [race] much thought. It's so hard to find someone that you really like that race isn't the issue. Actually, in the past I've dated mainly Caucasian and, I don't know, but to me it's like, it's so hard to find someone to begin with, that you can actually get along with, it's no big deal what race they are.

Times have certainly changed. What was taboo forty years ago for a woman Daphne's age is today a matter of personal inclination. Unlike Wilma, she does not feel constrained to choose from a pool of coethnics. Daphne's main concern is finding a compatible partner, and in her mind she is free to cross color as well as ethnic lines in search of this person. And cross she has—Daphne and other women younger than forty are more likely to date out than to date coethnics exclusively.

Young women such as Daphne are not the only ones dating outside of their ethnic group. Men we interviewed, particularly those under the age of forty, are pursuing outside love interests as freely as women. This is an important finding since it goes against earlier research suggesting that Asian-American men trail behind women in intermarriage and interdating behavior (Kitano et al., 1984; Spickard, 1989; Sung, 1990). Instead, it lends support to a trend detected by Shinagawa and Pang (1996) indicating that younger cohorts of native-born Chinese- and Japanese-American men are also expanding their pool of potential partners.

Since only four of the forty-eight single men and women we interviewed exclusively date coethnics, the question of whom the rest date naturally arises. Most date interracially (mostly commonly with whites) as well as interethnically (with other Asian-Americans). That they frequently choose white partners is not surprising because of the demographic dominance and availability of whites

(Sung, 1990). What is surprising, however, is how frequently they date other Asian-Americans, their casual attitudes about doing so, and in some cases, the purposefulness of their choices. Some, in fact, do not consider it interdating since, "after all, we're both Asian." Diane Okihiro, for example, spoke of the interchangeability in her mind between Chinese-American and Japanese-American men:

> I think most of the guys I've gone out with who are Chinese-American, the guy I'm with now, it's not any different. To me it's the same as being with someone who would be Japanese-American.

While at an earlier time a Japanese-American woman would have encountered stubborn resistance if she dated or married a Chinese-American man (remember Emily Woo's parents?), today this type of union hardly raises an eyebrow among contemporary and single Asian ethnics.

I believe the matter-of-fact attitude our respondents have toward interethnic dating is both the producer and product of an intense boundary shift currently taking place. More and more Asian ethnics, particularly younger ones, are defining themselves panethnically as Asian-Americans and identifying along racial lines (Espiritu, 1992; Onishi, 1996; Shinagawa & Pang, 1996). They subsequently can have a casual attitude because they believe it is still "within the family," the family of Asian-Americans, that is.

This has not come about easily nor naturally, however. Forces beyond the control of subsumed groups initially create panethnic categories, and the resulting label, in this case Asian-American, must first be externally imposed (Espiritu, 1992). Ignoring cultural, linguistic, and oftentimes longstanding animosity between different ethnic groups, members of the dominant society have historically invoked their power to categorize others according to criteria that are convenient for them (Nagel, 1991, 1994). This is how various indigenous tribal people have come to be identified as Indians and people from countries such as China, Japan, Vietnam, Korea, and the Philippines as Asian-Americans.

Only over time do groups who were forcibly lumped together (usually on the basis of shared language or presumed racial similarities) begin to recognize the commonalties in their experiences and form alliances to protect and promote their collective interests (Omi & Winant, 1994). Eventually, the identity that was originally imposed on them, in this case Asian-American, takes on a life and meaning of its own as a new cultural base reflecting their common experiences in the United States is gradually constructed (Nagel, 1991, 1994). Ethnic distinctions matter less and less in the face of an emerging racial consciousness (Onishi, 1996). This does not mean they cease to think of themselves in ethnic-specific terms as Chinese- or Japanese-American or that the panethnic progression is irreversible or even inevitable (Nagel, 1991, 1994).[1] The point to keep in mind is that they are more willing to see themselves as Asian-Americans in a larger variety of contexts.

Quite clearly, some respondents have made a conscious decision to date other Asians and do so for many reasons. Explanations ranged from wanting to please their parents to wishing to maintain a pure bloodline (interestingly, they do not equate interethnic dating with dilution). But the one reason most frequently given concerned the comfort and familiarity they felt interacting with other Asians. Gary Hong, who at an earlier time had dated white, black, and Latino women, shared why he now prefers Asian women:

> I have a preference for Asian Americans. Just because I find them more attractive to me. . . . I'm stereotyping but generally speaking, family backgrounds are compatible, we can do the same type of things. My parents would probably prefer me dating a Chinese or at least an Asian-American girl.

Nor was Gary the only who felt he had more in common with other Asian-Americans based on similar experiences, interests, and upbringing. Some who initially dated across racial lines discussed why they now preferred to date Asian-Americans. Marilyn Tokubo, for example, reflected on the attitude change that took place for her:

> Ever since college my preference has really been Asian.
> Q: Why?
> A: More comfortable. I don't have that [pause] I mean, I'd probably go out now since everything is personality for me. It's just that

most of the things I like to do are in this other circle. If he can assimilate to that then great, but most likely not.

College was clearly a pivotal time to develop an Asian-American preference. Coinciding with their own explorations into identity via courses in Asian-American studies (where many first began to think of themselves in panethnic terms) and racial/ethnic theory, they spoke of their amazement at meeting others who reminded them of themselves (Takagi, 1992). Particularly for those who grew up in predominantly white communities, college often provided the first opportunity to meet and interact with a large cross section of Asian-Americans. What they discovered were others who had grown up under similar circumstances and who therefore understood their experiences in a very personal way. This sense of familiarity and compatibility led some to their gradual preference for Asian-American friends and lovers.

From one perspective, our respondents' dating behavior may be viewed as further proof of the erosion of ethnicity's meaningfulness in their lives. Clearly, younger respondents do not feel constrained by social mores to date exclusively or eventually marry a coethnic. Because many have chosen to exercise their freedom of choice, their behavior could easily be interpreted as signaling the death knell for ethnicity as fewer and fewer homogeneous couples are formed and eventually sanctioned by marriage.

Viewed from a different perspective, however, their openness to dating other Asian-Americans can also be seen as an example of a new and thriving racial salience. Increasingly, the issue is not whether they date coethnics, but whether they date others within the same panethnic and racialized category as themselves.

I believe this embracement of a panethnic identity and consciousness represents the latest development in the evolution of their emergent identities and cultures. Ethnicity's influence in their lives has indeed shifted and changed, and for many racial considerations have replaced it.

As for the forty-seven respondents who are married, about one third have intermarried. Compared to the number of single respondents who have outdated, this number seems quite small. This figure is somewhat deceiving, however, since dating out and intermarrying are clearly more pronounced among younger Asian ethnics, particularly those who have attended college since the birth of the Asian-American student movement in the mid 1960s (Wei, 1993). Most of our married respondents are older than forty, thus skewing the figure toward homogeneous marriages.

For those who are intermarried, half are with white partners (except for one Chinese-American woman who is married to a Latino) and half with Asian-Americans. Interestingly, most respondents with a white spouse had almost exclusively dated whites before marrying their partner. Terry Winters, for instance, had never dated a Japanese-American man before marrying her white ethnic husband. Nor was this because of limited availability since she grew up in a diverse community in Los Angeles. Here she reflects on her dating history:

> Actually I've never dated a Japanese-American man. In high school I went out once with a guy who was Korean, [but] other than that I've only gone out with white guys.
>
> *Q:* Was that a conscious decision?
>
> *A:* They were the only guys I was attracted to, felt more comfortable with. I always would feel that Japanese guys [pause] I just wasn't what they were looking for, and they weren't what I was looking for either because I didn't fit into that conforming mold. I never kept up with all the things that were important to Japanese girls so I don't think I was desirable to them, that I was ever on the list. And all the guys liked the same girls. There'd really be like a list of who was most desirable. I'm too outspoken and too intimidating.

Terry's comments are reminiscent of a trend discussed in Chapter 3 in which some respondents consciously distanced themselves from other Asian-Americans to avoid being typecast. Terry mentioned a number of common stereotypes that she believed were true about Japanese-Americans and couched her uninterest in coethnic dating as being based on them. Not only did she consider herself different from the "typical" Japanese-American woman, she was not interested in dating the "typical" Japanese-American man. Respondents in Fong and Yung's (1997) study of Asian-Americans who dated and married white partners offered comments similar to Terry's. The "typical" Asian-American man or woman usually conformed to "typical" mainstream stereotypes.

As for those married to other Asian-Americans, their profiles resemble those of the single Asian ethnics who also expressed a pan-Asian dating preference. They either came to feel they shared more in common with other Asians (usually during college) or else had always traveled in Asian-American social circles and met their spouse in one of them.

Reweaving, Discarding, and Retaining Cultural Traditions: Childrearing in an Age of Abundant Choices

[I]f your Scandinavian mother painstakingly prepared seven kinds of fish for Christmas dinner and the thought of all those gills leaves you feeling limp, aim for capturing the essence of the meal—its specialness or ethnicity—rather than struggling to create a perfect replica, suggests Susan Abel Lieberman, author of *New Traditions: Redefining Celebration for Today's Family*. "Using the same threads, reweave the tradition to fit your lifestyle. Serve one kind of fish and read six Swedish poems," she says. "It's OK to change the rules." (Spencer, 1996, p. 167)

This passage vividly underscores the highly personal and voluntary nature of ethnic traditions for most American families. Parents may choose to promote their children's ethnic identities; they may not. Or, they may choose to modify whatever cultural practices they were raised with to suit their individual lifestyles as endorsed by the author above. Whatever the choice, one thing is clear; what was once a given—the tacit role of the family in transmitting cultural traditions to their children—has today become an option (Alba, 1990; Waters, 1990).

Our respondents who are parents have taken the advice offered in this passage to heart. They are quite open to creative reinterpretations of cultural traditions and are not overly concerned with their children's ethnic socialization. Joy Matsui expressed it best by saying, "Since I didn't grow up in that atmosphere, I won't go out of my way to learn about it. If the children want to, more power to them."

As their parents did for them, the strategy they prefer involves exposing their children to a range of cultural events and practices rather than forcing them to "come to the table." Morrison Hum,

> I think it is very important to know the identity, that you are Chinese-American. [But] accepting is personal. I don't push it on my kids . . . and my son doesn't pass it on to his kids. . . . We didn't teach them any Chinese. We tried to send them to Chinese school. It lasted a month maybe [laugh]. That was it. It's funny. She [daughter] has to be told that she is Chinese because we don't really do that much to remind her of her identity of being Chinese.

Parent after parent repeated this sentiment of wanting their children to choose their own ethnic path. While most do believe it is important to pass along some cultural knowledge, they feel the more crucial issue is to pass along a sense of Japanese or Chinese identity and for their children to be proud of this identity. Passing on traditional cultural practices seems to be less important since they are not particularly familiar with these practices.

When parents do feel a sense of obligation to play a more active role is during early adolescence since, as Dawn Chin put it, "children don't know about ethnicity and identity" at that age.[2] Dale Fujimoto, whose two daughters are currently in high school, described the efforts he and his wife made when they were younger:

> The only time we've really thought of it [being Japanese] consciously is when they were younger and there was more of a desire to create a force or be involved with other Japanese-Americans. We started with giving the girls the dolls that were put out and sent them to Japanese Bible school. My wife takes them to the Buddhist church. There was a time when we were a little bit more concerned with trying to emphasize the Japanese influence. Now I think we expose them to it but try to give them both sides. We've done a lot to at least try to give them some exposure.
>
> Q: And why is that important?

A: I think there is a cause to at least give them that exposure and the opportunity to explore. Just let them know it's not something they have to do but it is there if they choose to.

In addition to more traditional fare, our respondents also encouraged their children to participate in Americanized activities catering to Asian-Americans such as ethnic sports leagues and Girl/Boy Scout troops as their parents did for them. As their children became older, however, parents such as Dale lost much of the enthusiasm and sense of responsibility that had earlier motivated them. They had done their duty by providing their children with early opportunities to develop an interest; now it was up to the young people to pursue further knowledge.

Those with young children are currently in the parental phase that Dale and others with older children have exited. They are taking their kids to visit ethnic museums and exhibits, enrolling them in programs (sports leagues, karate/kung fu, church, or language school), and buying special toys and books. If the attitudes and behavior of the older parents is any indication, however, the enthusiasm and sense of duty younger parents currently feel is likely to taper off as their children grow.

For respondents with interethnic and interracial children, their hope is to expose them to both sides of their cultural background even though, as some acknowledge, greater emphasis may be placed on one side. Marie Nishida, who is married to a Chinese-American and has two children, acknowledged that Chinese influences run more strongly through her household:

> [Our life] it's more Chinese than Japanese I think. He's much closer to the Asian culture than I am. I mean I'm like a blank slate for American. Well, I mean there's some Japanese, but the way I'm Japanese is more like, I don't know, certain kinds of character make-up or sensibility. Just the way you deal with things. Whereas it's not like, this is our culture, we do this and that. Whereas he's very Chinese.

Similarly, Karen Flores conceded that her two young children probably receive more exposure to their Chinese ancestry because of their frequent interactions with her mother:

My husband's mother is not alive, and I don't know if you want to call it Chinese part, how strong the mother is in the Chinese family, but my mother is still alive, so my kids really know that they are Chinese, and they only like Chinese food, and they only know a little bit that they are Mexican right now.

As with homogeneous couples, however, parents of interracial and interethnic children still believe the decision to pursue further knowledge as well as how they will eventually identify belongs to their children. Their job is to expose them to both sides of their ancestry and then let them choose.

My main priority right now is raising my kids and instilling the Chinese things I know and learning about it is part of it. But they have another part of them that is Mexican and American. I take them to museums. I no sooner take them to the Asian Pacific Museum than the Museum of Natural History. I don't make a conscious effort [of] this is Chinese. . . . I want to expose my kids to it so if they take onto it, fine. If they don't . . .

For respondents without children the question of ethnic socialization is, of course, based on speculation since their attitudes may change once they become parents. At this stage, however, their feelings closely mirror those who are already parents. Again, the emphasis is on choice rather than forced learning.

[*Lonnie Wong*]: They would have to find out if being Chinese was real important to them.

[*Meg Takahashi*]: I think it's important. I think it's very important. At least they know that they appreciate what they have. But they should choose if they want to be more Japanese or a combination or just not follow it at all and be totally American and have nothing to do with Japanese culture.

[*Greg Okinaka*]: I would hope that they would just start on their own. You can't force them.

In short, most want their future children to be self-motivated and to develop a sincere interest in their ethnic history and culture *and to explore these on their own accord.* If they fail to do so, they, as parents, will not use a heavy hand to sway them.

▨ Summary

Our respondents have chosen not to integrate many traditional cultural elements into their lifestyles. They have not retained their ancestral language, do not celebrate ethnic holidays or events with much consistency or reverence, and despite good intentions are unlikely to follow through incorporating cultural traditions and values in their lives. As for their children, future or present, most believe the choice should be left to them whether or not they wish to live an ethnically inspired life. In short, sowing the seeds of interest by providing cultural stimuli early on, and then seeing if the seeds take root on their own is their preferred strategy.

Where our respondents do surprise, however, is in the area of dating, for a sizable number deliberately seek out other Asian-Americans to date. Even more surprising is the evolution taking place in their understanding of this behavior. Dating across ethnic lines is increasingly seen as a nonevent, as "something that everybody does." The boundaries that separated Asian ethnic groups in the past are becoming fuzzier as more people identify panethnically as Asian-Americans. The expansion of whom they are willing to identify with represents the latest modification to their emergent identities and cultures, a topic that I turn to next.

"I'm an American with a Japanese look"

CHAPTER 6

Emerging Identities and Practices

In the previous chapter I outlined the many ways ethnicity has ceased to be salient for our respondents. In this chapter I discuss the ways ethnicity has retained meaning in their lives. The cultural values and practices that are salient to them, however, are more Chinese-American, Japanese-American, and increasingly Asian-American in orientation than traditionally Chinese or Japanese. They were raised within emergent and hyphenated cultural environments, and it is to these that our respondents show genuine allegiance.

But there are also involuntary reasons why they continue to identify in ethnic and, increasingly, racial terms. Our respondents do not believe they have the option of doing away with ethnic or racial labels since these remain salient markers to others, influencing how they are defined, responded to, and treated. Furthermore, they believe the unhyphenated label, *American*, is reserved for describing white ethnics and would not be accepted by others if used to describe themselves. This belief is based on personal experiences with intentional prejudice, stereotyping, and a general perception that Asian-Americans are seen as a population composed of recent immigrants. This, in turn, has implications for their own attitudes and feelings toward Asian immigrants, a topic touched upon in previous chapters.

▨ "It doesn't make me any less of an Asian person because I can't speak the language": Evolving Cultural Values and Practices

Despite all of the ways ethnicity has ceased to influence their daily lives, our respondents do consider ethnicity a salient aspect of their identity. What matters to them, however, has increasingly little to do with cultural traditions as practiced by Chinese and Japanese nationals. Instead, their focus rests squarely on the evolving cultural patterns being generated in this society by Japanese-American, Chinese-American, and other Asian-American groups. The cultural elements they feel are worth retaining are the emergent as well as reinterpreted values and practices they grew up with that weave together strands of Japanese, Chinese, and American mainstream cultures. Lisa Lowe (1996) speaks to this theme when she writes: "The making of Asian American culture includes practices that are partly inherited, partly modified, as well as partly invented" (p. 65).

Greg Okinaka, a Sansei in his twenties, was particularly insightful about the dynamic character of culture. He describes his philosophy here:

> I mean, I think it is very important for the next generation, the younger, the next bunch of people to realize . . . I think there's such a specific Japanese, no, not Japanese, well, Asian-American [pause] culture that has evolved and that is in the process of evolving [and] that it's more important to learn about that than it is to learn about . . . I mean because the Asia, the Japan that my parents knew when they were my age was a completely different Japan than I know at my current age. And it's gonna be a different Japan that any other generations learn fifteen or twenty years from now.

Greg is speaking of a "homegrown" culture and identity that reflect the cultural frames of reference influencing his life, and his pride as well as defensiveness about that developing identity are important features. It is more important, he thinks, to be well versed in the culture that is evolving here in the United States (which is increasingly panethnic in orientation) than in Japan's culture, a value he acquired from his parents and continues to uphold in his own life.

Greg's interpretation of culture as a dynamic medium was shared by many others. Gary Hong, for instance, was only interested in maintaining cultural practices that held meaning for him:

> In culture I basically [pause] it's important. But the traditions, I'm not into doing customs just for the sake of doing customs. That's sort of silly. Just because they've been around for a long time that people do it. Like lighting incense and bowing three times. Just because they do it for the hell of it doesn't mean a damn thing to me. I could really care less. I think it's important to be educated, to know why people do it and to know that people do it.

Similarly, while Jan Muramoto acknowledged she would like to know more about Japanese cultural traditions, it did not make her any "less Asian" simply because she did not:

> I took three years of Spanish to qualify for college because it was easier, and you know, people say to me all the time, don't you feel guilty? And I say, you know, you can't live your life feeling guilty. It doesn't make me any less of an Asian person because I can't speak the language. It doesn't make me any less of a person because I don't make sushi. There are other things that I teach my children. I mean my parents didn't speak Japanese at home. They spoke English to us. . . . We speak English at home. We live in this country. We speak English.

Jan is clearly defensive about her authenticity as an "Asian person" because she has been challenged on this issue before. She is rebelling against a static definition that stipulates that unless she is fluent in Japanese and can make sushi, she is not "really Japanese." She prefers a more fluid interpretation of culture since that is how she was brought up to understand it herself.

"When I'm with my Caucasian friends it seems like there's less in common": A Preference for Asian-American and Coethnic Friends

One cultural value modified to reflect the boundary shifts taking place among different Asian ethnic groups includes their preference for ethnic friendships. While clearly not a new cultural value, our respondents have put their own twist on it by expanding the category panethnically to include Asian-Americans more generally. Less than a fifth described their friends as consisting exclusively of coethnics, but more than a third have friendship circles consisting primarily of other Asian-Americans; the remainder describe their friends as racially diverse or primarily white.

Those with predominantly Asian-American friends claim to share a special bond or sense of kinship with them that they do not necessarily experience with non-Asians. Barry Sato,

> It was easier to hang out with Asians. Thing is when you talk about things your experiences and values seem to mesh a little bit more.

References were repeatedly made to perceived similarities between themselves and their Asian-American friends based on similar upbringing, parental expectations, values, and even experiences with stereotyping and intentional prejudice, discrimination, and marginalization. These shared experiences, as Laura Nee remarked, result in comfortable interactions: "There's less explaining because we were brought up pretty much the same." Whereas in the past this sentiment would have extended only to coethnics, today it increasingly applies to other Asian-Americans irrespective of ethnicity, a finding that concurs with their attitudes toward interethnic dating and marriage discussed in the previous chapter. This sense of camaraderie does not extend to Asian immigrants, however, unless they are far along in their acculturation process, as will be discussed below.

Since most live in racially diverse or predominantly white communities, the question of where these friendships develop naturally arises. Some were forged during their youth in school, sports leagues, church, and the neighborhood. It seems the efforts of their parents years earlier did not go to waste since close friendships were formed in the very places their families hoped they would. As adults, they meet other Asian-Americans in a variety of settings. Because of their concentration in the San Francisco and Los Angeles areas, they do not need to look very far to find Asian-Americans.

As often happened during their childhood, the activities they engage in with their Asian-American friends are not ethnically centered in any traditional sense. As later generation Americans, they are highly acculturated and participate in many of the same activities as other Californians despite race or ethnicity. About a third are members of one or more organized ethnic activities. Especially popular among younger respondents are Asian-American sports leagues from which there are myriad to choose: J.A.V.A. (Japanese-American Volleyball Association), the Westside Volleyball League, and the L.A. Asian Ski Club, to name only a few. Some have also joined college fraternities and sororities and other campus groups geared toward Asian-American students. For professionals, a wide range of business networks and employee associations where mg berfl share both classes and ethnic resources (e.g., Asian Professional Exchange [A.P.E.X.], Asian Business League [A.B.L], Asian-American Journalist Association, Young Generation Asian Professionals [Y.G.A.], Asian Business Association [A.B.A.], M Society, and Orange County Chinese-American Chamber of Commerce) is available. Vo's (1996) research, for example, on the San Diego branch of the A.B.A. explains how members develop business opportunities and deal with issues such as glass ceilings in the workplace and trade with the Pacific Rim. And, of course, membership in long-standing political interest groups such as the Japanese American Citizens League (J.A.C.L.) and the Organization of Chinese Americans (O.C.A.) is common, as is church attendance in predominantly Asian congregations.

In this sense, our respondents are carrying on a tradition dating back to an earlier period of racism and social exclusion. Because native-born Asian-Americans were barred from participating in mainstream clubs and activities with white children, community leaders took it upon themselves to sponsor their own chapters and clubs to meet their children's needs (Chan, 1991b). Many of these clubs have survived to the present day and, while no longer forced to participate in ethnically specific leagues, many choose to do so out of family tradition or sense of comfort.

Wiener Teriyaki, The Culinary Future?

Another cultural value that has been maintained yet also altered is an appreciation for ethnic food. Despite some drop-off, a surprisingly resilient number continue to eat some version of Chinese or Japanese food on a regular or semiregular basis. While a few still put in the effort to cook "authentic" meals, most simply go to restaurants. Carol Wong prepares Chinese food more regularly than others, but acknowledged that the abundant availability of Chinese restaurants in the Bay Area was a real bonus:

> I cook Chinese food around three times a week. But we go out to eat. I mean, around here you can go out. So we have to choose like what do we want. Do we want Little Hong Kong? Do we want Sun Hong Kong? Do we want Little Golden Dynasty for down home Cantonese cooking?

Not only are they free to sample different regional cuisines within one ethnicity (in Carol's case, Chinese), they can easily explore the foods of different Asian groups (Thai, Korean, Filipino, Lao, Hmong, Vietnamese, Malaysian, Singaporean, Cambodian). The gastronomic possibilities are endless. By virtue of living in the San Francisco Bay Area and southern California, areas with the largest and most diverse Asian populations in the United States and, thus, best selection of restaurants, they have the good fortune to be able to sample from a wide range of authentic cuisines.

More commonly, however, they prepare quick and novel versions of ethnic dishes or use Asian ingredients to make what would otherwise be American dishes. The most common complaint for not cooking traditional dishes is the time and difficulty involved in preparing quality Chinese or Japanese food. Nevertheless, preferences for certain Chinese and Japanese spices, sauces, and condiments they grew up eating are hard to quell. This is why during a last-minute rush to prepare a meal, they are more inclined to grab a bottle of soy sauce rather than steak sauce to pour over some hamburger. They are continuing a practice started by their parents and kin of modifying ethnic dishes to fit their lifestyles and food tastes.

Rice continues to be a staple food for many, although even here there is evidence of change. Laura Hong, a fifth-generation Chinese-American, provides an example: "We always have Chinese rice at [my parents'] home, but I have a lot of Japanese friends who eat sticky rice so, and I like sticky rice so I make that more." As our respondents are moving toward embracing a panethnic identity and befriending other Asian-Americans, they are also sampling other cuisines and expanding their taste preferences. Arnie Kumamoto and his Japanese-American wife, for example, are just as likely to prepare stir-fry meals in a wok, traditionally considered a Chinese practice, as they are to prepare Japanese food:

> My wife and I eat [Japanese] about twice a week. But see, it's not considered real Japanese food like people you expect from Japan to eat. I think we kind of eat, we mix things around. We throw on the Chinese food and the Japanese food and throw on a steak or something. We do a lot of stir-fry. The steaks are always stir-fry. We cook things out of a wok. Most of the time we eat steamed rice instead of bread. We have that for breakfast with eggs, etc. But it's a little hard to say what's Japanese. . . . Sometimes we get some sushi and have it, eat out late and have some [pause] soup that would be Japanese [pause] but a lot we just mix things.

This passage nicely captures the mixing and melding taking place for this young couple as they carve out a lifestyle of their own. Arnie and his wife feel at ease in reinterpreting, combining, and borrowing from a variety of culinary sources. Some Japanese elements have been retained, some Chinese elements added, and some American influences (steak) modified to suit their individual preferences.

"I'm not your typical American when people think American": Identity Options and Constraints

A third cultural value our respondents adhere to comes as no surprise in light of what has been discussed in previous chapters. They believe that having pride in their emerging identities is more important than to be knowledgeable of cultural traditions, a theme that has also surfaced in studies of white ethnicity (Alba, 1990; Gans, 1979; Kellogg, 1990; Waters, 1990).

Whereas whites can capriciously base identity choices on nothing more than "a sense that it is nicer to be an X, rather than a Y" (Alba, 1990, p. 62), the choices available to Asian ethnics are markedly more circumscribed. Most identify in hyphenated terms as Chinese-American, Japanese-American, and, increasingly, Asian-American. Cathy Leong, who identifies as an Asian-American, explained her choice:

> For myself I have more Japanese, Korean, Filipino friends, just through work and the people we associate with, you know, my co-workers and stuff like that. So I think there's more of an emphasis on Asian-American.

As more individuals come to think of themselves as members of a general family of Asian-Americans and associate accordingly, they are more likely to embrace the panethnic label to describe themselves. Since the bulk of her friends are other Asians, Cathy feels more comfortable reinforcing the bond between them all, their common race, and thus downplaying ethnic differences.

Emily Woo, who also identifies as an Asian-American, does so because it encompasses both her Chinese and Japanese roots:

Q: How do you identify yourself?
A: That's a really hard question actually. I guess as an Asian-American. I don't consider myself just Japanese, just Chinese. I don't consider myself just American. I don't know. I kinda like terminology like Asian-American and African-American because it's kinda messy. . . . By blood, I'm Chinese and Japanese. By culture, I don't know if I am so much of either. I don't know. . . . Mom would always tell me I used to get confused growing up. "How can I be Japanese and Chinese and American?" "Well, you are half Japanese, half Chinese, and all American."

For Emily, identifying along racial lines as an Asian-American eliminates the cumbersome task of acknowledging both components of her ancestry. Her rationale allows a glimpse into how future generations of mixed ancestry Asians may possibly identify.

Tony Lam, also of Chinese and Japanese ancestry, prefers to call himself an American-Asian. As the son of a career soldier and a veteran himself, he chooses to emphasize his patriotism to this country by asserting his American identity first. Yet, Tony also expressed great frustration over what could be characterized as a societal "blind spot" to the role Asian-Americans have played in this country:

Q: How do you identify yourself?

A: American-Asian. . . . I saw that parade in '92 on Hollywood Boulevard and they had veterans marching down [pause] I tell you which group was missing. Asian. There was not one Chinese, Japanese, Filipino, Korean, Pacific Islander in uniform. Now I know they served [pause]. It's either the fault of those people who plan that parade or the fault due to a lack of vigilance for an Asian veterans organization by not insisting on it [pause] through all that hard times. I still persist that I'm an American, but I'm not going to deny that I'm Asian because first thing they're not going to let me do it. I still got to [pause] about Asian culture whether I like it or not. . . . You see, Caucasians must understand that they [pause] put that on us, and we must learn to confront people who say those kinds of things so we should say things like, "No I don't know that, I hope you know your French food. Or, he's Scottish [pause] look, look, what are you? Okay, Armenian. Tell me about Armenian stuff. We should put that on them. I think it's fair, they got to get a taste of what they did or how dumb they sound or who's truly American. Yeah, I am American and then Asian.

Tony considers himself to be a loyal American who risked his life to defend his country. The irony, however, is that there are others do not consider the United States to be his country. Even if he chose to identify solely as an American, he believes "they," presumably white Americans, would not legitimate his choice— "they're not going to let me do it."

Others also spoke about the pressures they experienced to identify in ethnic or racial terms. Ted Uyematsu:

Q: How about identifying as just a plain old American?

A: Yeah I would, but you know [pause] there's [pause] but then again you have to realize that I'm not your typical American when people think American. In your mind you don't see a whole-blooded Japanese guy you know. They conjure up some blond-headed dude that [pause] but I would have no problem seeing myself but I think it would confuse certain people if I were to say that.

Ted shows a clear understanding of what the typical American male presumably looks like—and he does not even come close. Subsequently, while he had no qualms calling himself an American, Ted believed others might take issue with him since he feels white ethnics feel a sense of proprietary claim to the term. As such, he was unsure how his usage of the term would be received.

As a compromise, most have chosen a hyphenated identity to honor their American as well as ethnic roots. Victor Ong spoke insightfully about his decision to call himself a Chinese-American:

Usually I say Chinese-American because I realize I'm not Chinese. People from China come over here and like, whoa, they're like a foreign species. And I'm not American because just one look and I'm apart. I used to struggle with this question a lot and to make a long story short, Chinese-American is a hybrid of its own. It's kind of like Afro-Americans. Boy, they're not African and they're not American, and it's just its own species, and that's the way it is.

Victor did not feel comfortable describing himself in strictly ethnic terms as Chinese because he does not identify with Chinese immigrants. But he also sensed that identifying solely as an American was problematic—he did not believe that others would accept his choice since "just one look and I'm apart." In other words, he believed his physical features did not conform to commonly accepted notions of what a "real" American looked like.

Others were even more direct in stating how inappropriate *in other people's eyes* it would be if they were to identify as Americans without any hyphenation. Rick Wubara and Kevin Fong explain why they identify as Japanese-American and Chinese-American, respectively:

[*Rick*]: I don't think I can be just American just for the fact that I look different from the typical American, white. [Why not just Japanese then?] Because I definitely am Americanized, an American raised in America. And I don't always agree with what Japanese, Japan stands for.

[*Kevin*]: First and foremost I was born Chinese, and this goes back to what my brother told me one time. He said, and I totally related with that, "You're born Chinese, but when you're around Chinese people, like when I'm around real Chinese people, they don't think I'm Chinese because I was born here, and I'm kind of Americanized. And if I call myself an American, I hang around with American guys, they don't consider me American because I don't look American, I'm Chinese. So I would say that I'm Chinese-American first and foremost. I was born Chinese, and I'm proud of that but I'm also proud that I'm an American of the United States.

"I don't look American." "I'm not your typical American." "I'm not Chinese . . . and I'm not American." These statements vividly convey the dilemma our respondents, as racialized ethnics, face. They have learned by watching how others respond to them that this society views them as outsiders. Despite being longtime Americans, they are not perceived as such since they do not fit the image of what a "real" American looks like (Espiritu, 1992; Jiobu, 1988; Lowe, 1996; Nagel, 1994). This, I believe, is the key difference separating the white ethnic from the Asian ethnic experience. While white ethnics must actively assert their ethnic uniqueness if they wish this to feature prominently in their interactions with others, Asian ethnics are assumed to be foreign unless proven otherwise.

▨ *"That's when I knew I was Chinese": The Realization of Difference*

No one ever asks a Polish American after the first generation why they don't speak Polish or are they ashamed of being Polish because they don't speak Polish. But [they will say] that you're ashamed of being Chinese, or you don't understand Chinese culture because you don't speak Chinese. But no one ever asks that of anybody else. I mean if your grandparents speak French, and you still cook coq au vin, but no one ever demands that you also know how to speak French. And no one ever asks you, where did you come from.

The frustration Carol Wong experiences is hard to miss in this passage. She believes a double standard is operating. While white ethnics are free to discard their ethnic links and merge with the American mainstream after the first generation, Asian ethnics do not have this option; an assumption of foreignness stubbornly clings to them despite generational status.

Carol was not alone in her way of thinking. Others concurred with her assessment of the status difference between Asians and whites. Based on their experiences with prejudice, discrimination, and stereotyping, they understand that the public is unable or unwilling to distinguish between Asian ethnics and immigrants. That our respondents, residents of such diverse and cosmopolitan areas as Los Angeles and San Francisco, still feel this way is telling. Subsequently, our respondents believe their status in this society is vulnerable to changing social, political, and economic conditions beyond their personal control (Nishi, 1989). For instance, the majority agree their lives would be effected not only if the United States was to go to war with their country of origin but if war was declared on *any* Asian country since "whites or blacks can't tell the difference between Asian-Americans and Asians." Carol Wong again:

> When there was all the whoop-de-do about Japan and all the businesses that Japan owns and all the property that Japan owns in this country, [while] England, Canada, and the Netherlands own a whole lot more individually than Japan ever did. But it was this thing of the Pacific horde. And of course American car companies screwed up, and they had to blame it on someone else.

Respondents frequently made references to Japan and Middle Eastern "bashing" as well as the wartime internment of Japanese-Americans to substantiate their views. And while not everybody believed that a mass internment sanctioned by the federal government could happen again, most agreed that hostilities from the general citizenry were likely. Friends and co-workers who knew them as individuals probably would not act differently, but strangers and nativists certainly would. As Jonathan Tse put it, "They'd see us as being evil, and they'd start, it's just like what they do with the Middle East and the Soviet Union. They would all look down on us."

Would the lives of white ethnics be affected if war was declared on their country or countries of origin? Most answered no. Morrison Hum, who was required to wear a badge identifying himself as Chinese during World War II, looked to the past to substantiate his opinion:

Q: If [the] U.S. were to go to war with Europe . . .
A: Probably not, because they are considered white. I don't believe so. Like the Germans [pause] but you stand out because you are colored. It would make you feel bad too. Feel ashamed of your native country.

Whiteness, once again, is equated with being American; Asianness is not. And because Asianness is not, questions regarding their loyalty to this country are raised. This was the case during World War II, and many of our respondents believe this is still the case today. Daphne Kitano,

Q: If [the] U.S. were to go to war with Europe . . .
A: No, because it didn't really happen to Germans in World War II, and they were our enemies, and the Italians were our enemy, and it didn't happen to them, you know, which leads me to believe the obvious, that it was just on the basis of color of your skin. If you weren't white, and you were Japanese, and even though you were American, you were still the enemy. . . . I still feel there's some trend that the media is generating about how Japanese are taking over the United States or buying out everything, which is totally not the real case. They're not looking at the investments that England has in the United States, or the Canadians or Australians, the Dutch, the Germans. And I was like, you know, the media say all these things about Japanese taking over and it [pause] it's going to affect me here, a Japanese-American, because the ignorant white person isn't going to [pause] it's going to be

like, "Oh you're just one of those Japanese who are trying to take over." So they don't realize the effect, the effect on how people view Asians in this country.

As for the possibility of another mass internment, opinions were mixed. About one third did not believe it could happen again. Some felt the country had learned its lesson and would not repeat the mistakes made with Japanese-Americans. References were made to how "times have changed," as indicated by interest in multicultural issues and greater respect for human rights. Others referred to the growing political power of Asian-American organizations that would fight against such actions. Still a third response, captured by Greg Okinaka's comments, suggests that the imprisonment of the spirit may be more damaging than that of the flesh:

> I don't think they'd be sending mass people to prison, but if something like a war came up with the Japanese, you would be getting a lot more widespread discrimination. It's more like a mental internment than an actual physical internment, understand?

The rest either conceded internment was possible but unlikely or adamantly agreed that mass incarceration was not only possible but probable if the political situation became volatile enough.

In response to the question, "Does it mean something different to say you are an American of Irish (or any European ethnicity) descent compared to saying you are an American of Chinese or Japanese descent?" Morrison Hum had this to say:

> Yeah, there is a difference. They still look at the Chinese as a foreigner. For an Irish-American, they don't see him as a foreigner. I don't know how long it is going to take, but you are still looked upon as a foreigner. I think so.

Diane Okihiro chose to personalize the question by applying it to her Irish-American girlfriend and herself. Her response is revealing:

> Like my girlfriend, it's kinda funny because she's of Irish descent, but people would never think that or ask where are you from because they see her as being Caucasian. And if they look at me they would say, "Oh where are you from," because I'm

perceived as being Asian first. It's like girl, an Asian girl, and anything that follows after that. For my girlfriend it would be like, she's white, she's of Irish descent but it doesn't really matter. It's like way down the list of whatever.

Here Diane refers to her racial distinctiveness as featuring prominently in her interactions with strangers; she believes it is the first aspect of her identity to register with others. This, in turn, triggers an assumption of being from somewhere else, since being Asian is not equated with being from the United States. No one ever thinks to ask her girlfriend of Irish ancestry where she is from, however, because of her white racial background combined with a high degree of acculturation.

"Where are you really from?": Playing the Ethnic Game

Most of our respondents have been asked the question, "Where are you from?" at some point in their lives. All have learned that the question really being asked is, "What is your ancestral homeland?" since answering "San Jose" or "Los Angeles" usually fails to satisfy whoever is asking. Such a localized answer typically results in the response, "No. Where are you *really* from?" While some answer straightforwardly, others choose to play an "ethnic game" with their interrogator. This involves mischievously bantering with whomever is asking the question until the that person gives up or refine their query. Dani Murayama's and Greg Okinaka's experiences provide excellent examples:

[*Dani*]: A lot of times people will come up to me, and ask me where I'm from, and I'll answer Los Angeles, and they'll look at me really strange [laugh]. But that's where I'm from, and then they'll say, "No, no, no. Where were you born?" And I'll say Los Angeles. And then they'll ask me where my parents were born, and I'll tell them the United States. And then they'll ask me where my grandparents were born, and I'll tell them the United States [laugh].

[*Greg*]: I get it all the time. I think it's kind of funny because I always say, "I'm from so and so." And then they say, "No. Where are you from?" And then you say, "Well, actually I'm from Oakland." "No. Where are you *from*?" "And then it's like, "Well, I'm from North Dakota, if you want to go there." Then it's like, "No, no, no . . . " [laugh].

What strikes me about these passages is the insistence on the part of their interrogators to get to the *truth*, to find out where Dani and Greg are *really* from. They were not satisfied with the responses provided because they believed these two had to come from some place other than this country. Dani and Greg, for their parts, were only willing to provide opaque answers as a gesture of defiance.

Tony Lam, who also plays the ethnic game, refuses to give others the satisfaction of pigeonholing him as a foreigner to this country:

> Yeah, I get that all the time. You know what I tell them? I use the tact now. This guy [was] asking me and I could tell he's really excited [and] he's anticipating the answer. "Will it be Thailand? Will it be Japan?" He's all excited. Maybe he went to the Orient. And I tell him with a perfect look, "San Jose." And all of a sudden he has all this enthusiasm, flustered and goes, "Oh, San Jose." I'm answering honestly where I came from.

Some might think Tony, Dani, and Greg are being unnecessarily cheeky and too sensitive to a seemingly innocuous question. After repeatedly facing this line of questioning, however, they have grown impatient with others' needs to categorize them. After all, the answers they provide are truthful given what is being asked. Where are they from? They are from this country, as are their parents, and, in some cases, their grandparents and great-grandparents.

"Gee, your English is so good": Other Popular Stereotypes

A related stereotype our respondents encounter is an assumption of Chinese or Japanese language fluency and its corollary, surprise over their fluency in English. As Terry Winters put it, "I've had this happen all my life when some stranger will come up and start speaking Japanese to me, and I don't speak Japanese." Women, in particular, were more likely to recall instances where unsolicited male strangers approached with the intent of "hitting" on them or otherwise engaging them in conversation. Marilyn Tokubo,

> I get offended, and then there's times when somebody will come up to me in a bar and say, "Are you Japanese," and start speaking Japanese to me and actually [pause] people do this to me all the time, and I don't know why it's me over anybody else. They always seem to zoom in on me and start speaking this, trying to speak Japanese.
>
> Q: Who approaches you?
>
> A: Whites. They'll come up and start gibber jabbering in Japanese, and I'll just kind of have to laugh it off, and this happens a lot, and also that they assume that I know how to speak Japanese, and they also want to show off their Japanese.

Far from flattering, Marilyn experiences these instances as invasions into her privacy and resents the arrogance these men display in assuming they are welcome to approach her. Popular racialized and gendered stereotypes such as the "Suzie Wong" character portraying Asian women as subservient, acquiescent, sensual, and exotic have encouraged white men in particular to view her as an object for their entertainment (Fong, 1998; Hamamoto, 1994; Kim, 1986). Also at play in situations such as these is the element of white male privilege, the sense of entitlement those in the "driver's seat" feel whether consciously or not.

Other types of language stereotypes abound. Michael Lowe, a manager for a chain electronics store in the Bay Area, deals with irate customers all of the time. After soothing one woman who called to complain about the purchase of a faulty CD player she exclaimed, "Thank God you're an American! I'm tired of dealing with all those ching chong people!" Another respondent, Barry Sato, who spends a large portion of his day on the phone with clients, struggles with the preconceived notions of those he does business with and their subsequent reactions when they meet in person:

> I think a couple of times my jaws hit the ground. Why should my English be any different? . . . Mostly I was shocked. When

> I met someone who I've talked on the phone with, and when they saw me they'll go, "I didn't realize you were Asian." That was the first time. I was shocked. And on the other side when I met them what I really want to say was, "Oh, I couldn't tell you were black over the phone either." But I held my tongue because now let's not have a fight [laugh].

Without the benefit of sight or knowledge of his last name, Barry's client was surprised to learn he had been conducting business with a Japanese-American. Barry has since become used to this kind of response from his clients. He claims it does not bother him anymore; he just shakes his head in amazement over the regularity with which people cannot believe that he doesn't "sound" Japanese over the phone.

For the most part, the stereotyping our respondents experience is not intended to wound or alienate. Rather, incidents are largely based on the ignorance of generally well-intentioned people. Even when no ill will is intended, however, hurt is inflicted since, once again, they are reminded that they are viewed not as individuals but as stereotyped members of a group relegated to a foreign status. The frustration comes from trying so hard to be treated as a distinct individual and then confronting a thoughtless stereotype. Tony Lam,

> My closest friend happens to be Caucasian. He says, Tony, you're a good old boy like me, you know. You're just Asian on the outside, but you like burgers and so forth and all that. I told him I like Caucasian women, they look pretty good to me, you know, everybody else, I like Asian too. . . . So how does he see me? He sees me as an American but sometimes he has to make offhanded comments like, "Aah So," or something like that, and I go why do you have to bring that for? I don't go up to you and say you want to go dance country with all the other rednecks. Why can't we just be neutral?

"You feel like they're staring at you": Feeling Out of Place

Yet another way our respondents are reminded of their marginalized status concerns the stares, comments, and even threats they

receive from others who look upon them as strangers or intrud-
ers; about half have felt out of place or suddenly conscious of their
racial background during a stop somewhere. Most often this oc-
curs when they travel or visit unfamiliar places but this also happens in their own neighborhoods. I recently experienced an
example of this while making a supermarket stop in the city of San
Marino, an affluent suburb in southern California where recently
many well-to-do Chinese immigrants have moved. While standing
in line to pay for my items, two older white women behind me
began to complain about how Asians were taking over the area.
Neither woman appeared particularly concerned that I, an Asian
woman, could hear everything they were saying; they either assumed I could not speak English or did not care in the least.

The experience of walking into a restaurant ("a McDonald's
in the middle of nowhere") and having all heads turn to watch them
was a familiar story. Sharon Young,

> [T]here are times when you go to a restaurant, or you go some-
> where like a business or something, and you walk in, and
> they're all Caucasians. I don't know if it's unconscious or what,
> but you feel like they're staring at you, or they're looking, or
> they notice. Even coming down my street sometimes which
> basically is all white, and we've all lived here for years, and
> still when we drive they all kinda stare at you like, "Oh my
> gosh, they're Asian." Like we used to experience that a lot
> when we went to the market, and we'd go there and get all
> these stares, people would look at you. And you first think,
> "Haven't you seen an Asian in your life?" God, just because
> you have dark hair and different skin, it's like, wake up, you
> know. It's occasional, but it's still kinda sad because you still
> feel that.

Feeling uncomfortable while stopping in gas stations, gift shops,
and other stores was also frequently mentioned as was receiving
poor service. In all of these cases, the message they received was
that they were out of "place" or clearly did not belong where they
were. In some cases, local residents were merely confused over
their presence and viewed them as oddities. In other cases, hostility was unmistakable. Tony Lam,

I passed this car, these two Caucasians were in the car. They were slow, and I just passed them, and they notice[d] that I was Asian and drove alongside me. We drove through the entire town, side-by-side, and then they tried to hit me. At first they called me names, and I rolled my window up. So then he set himself on the window of the passenger side and started to give me the finger, and I ignored it and drive down the road. . . . They tried to run me off, hit me, I guess. So I sped up and got to a four-corner stop . . . and I look up, and I saw the driver there, but where is the other fella? And I find out what he was doing. He grabbed a bottle, and now he is sitting himself on the window and trying to position himself so that when they got near me, he could throw the bottle. I turn my lights on. They thought I was braking, and they suddenly brake and threw the bottle and miss, and I drove through the lights. I drove through the stop sign taking a risk of I might be hit or arrested by the police.

Similarly, Paul Leong described the unease he felt while working in a rural part of California. While he never experienced anything close to what Tony Lam endured, he maintained an alert stance during his time there:

When I worked in Sacramento, we used to go to different places in the Valley, like all white towns and stuff like that, quite a bit. And you do feel kinda conscious about how they're gonna treat you and that kind of thing, and I think it actually has maybe socially hindered me in some ways. But I also [pause] it's a safety mechanism because you never know what's going to happen. You're out there in the middle of farmland U.S.A. and shit. You never know if Joe Bob's gonna come around the corner with a rake and shit. It's never happened yet, but I do feel very sensitive about that.

Women traveling to unfamiliar places typically encountered gendered stereotypes that were used to make sense of their presence. Patti Ito, "When I've gone to places like Oklahoma, you know, I kind of feel like they think I'm some sort of Korean bride that some army person brought back." Again, the point is that some special explanation is needed to placate local residents as to why there are "strangers" in their community.

For their psychological as well as physical survival, our respondents have honed their sensory skills to a finely tuned level. Upon entering an unfamiliar environment, their "antennae" come out looking for any signs of potential trouble and gauging the degree of safety. The price paid for such attentiveness, however, is high. As Paul Leong mentioned earlier, he has socially hindered himself by being on the lookout for trouble so intently. And yet, he feels compelled to do so because he knows in some communities his presence is not welcome.

"It gives us Asian-Americans a bad name": Intolerance toward Asian Immigrants

One damaging consequence to come from the realization of their marginalized status concerns our respondents' attitudes toward Asian immigrants. Anti-immigrant sentiment runs high since immigrants are seen as fueling the stereotypes that have contributed to their conditional status as "honorary" but not "legitimate" Americans. Because most non-Asians cannot distinguish between Asian ethnics and immigrants, their destinies, for better or worse, are inexorably linked. Jerry Fong,

Q: Does their [Asian immigrants] presence affect your life in any way?

A: Yeah, it definitely does because of the prevalence again. Once again this yellow peril type thing where the people are seeing these large concentrations of Asian immigrants just because of the fact we all look alike, we're all Asian. They'll confuse me even though I may dress American. They'll still think I'm a foreigner. I've heard, "Why don't you go home," and stuff like that. So it does affect me.

As Jerry's comments suggest, most believe it is for the worse since their high visibility and larger numbers inevitably "distort the view of all Asians." Eileen Inouye's comments capture the sentiments of many:

Q: Does their [immigrants] presence affect the lives of people like yourself who have lived here for many generations, in any way?

A: Yeah, I think so. Because when the general public is very anti-immigrant, how can they distinguish if you're an immigrant or not? Based on what you look like? Or are they going to wait until you speak and figure out how bad your accent is? There's no way to tell besides looking and saying you're obviously a non-Caucasian, you must be an immigrant. It does affect all of our lives no matter who we are or what we do. Judge Lance Ito gets this all the time. He doesn't speak with an accent. He grew up here. He's very American, but when they deal with him in the media, it just really affects [pause] I think that one book that somebody put out [pause] O. J. Simpson himself. I think it was very damaging. Like Judge Ito, they made fun of his Japanese background.

Eileen's comments are in reference to the D'Amato-Ito incident discussed in Chapter 1 and bring home the point of the interwoven fates of immigrant and native-born Asians. Immigrants are seen as complicating the status of Asian ethnics in this society by reinforcing the very stereotypes they struggle so hard to avoid. These include being: clannish, selfish, rude, aggressive, unwilling to assimilate, nerdy, and overachieving. Rather than directing their resentment at the perpetrators and creators of these stereotypes, however, they are more likely to get angry at those whom they see as fueling the stereotypes.

Recent tensions in the southern California community of Monterey Park, "America's first suburban Chinatown," are exemplary of the bad blood that exists between immigrant and native-born Asians (Fong, 1994; Horton, 1995; Saito, 1993). As wealthy Chinese immigrants began pouring into the community in the 1970s, fears of a "take-over" were triggered; many local citizens, Asian and non-Asian alike, experienced their presence as an unwelcome intrusion. With their significant class resources ("I swear, they all drive Mercedes Benzes"), Chinese immigrants aggressively set out to make the city a more livable place for themselves, including installing Chinese business signs. Some business owners failed to include English subtitles, however, outraging local residents who took this action as an arrogant affront. They resented what they saw as the immigrants' unwillingness to assimilate quickly or quietly. Local Asian ethnics, meanwhile, suffered from the actions of their immigrant counterparts; after years of carefully cultivating good relations with their non-Asian neighbors, they found themselves subject to the same hostilities as immigrants (Horton, 1995; Saito, 1993). In response, many became the harshest critics of the immigrants whom they saw as spoiling what they had worked so hard to establish—a positive image.

Nor is Monterey Park the only place where such tensions have developed. Asian ethnics everywhere have felt squeezed by the presence of Asian immigrants. In San Francisco, where the class background of recent arrivals is less ostentatious, the complaint is that immigrants are uncouth and pushy. Andrew Lee,

Q: Do Chinese immigrants affect your life?

A: I think in terms personally, stereotypically, what they do outwardly. It gives the stereotype that there are more of these people doing these things, that all Chinese must spit on the street. All Chinese people must push on the bus.

Whether the stereotypes center around wealth or poverty, pushiness or submissiveness, overachievers or gangbangers, immigrants have become easy targets for our respondents' frustrations. Peggy Endo,

I remember my son Ken was coming back from a football game, and they were stopped by the San Marino police. They weren't doing anything. They were just Asian. And the first thing they said to them was, "Do you speak English?" And they have more often than not been stopped and questioned, and I don't know if you can call it harassed because they have just lumped all Asians that are immigrants, rich, taking advantage of America and communities and not giving back to the community. Just taking, etc. etc. I mean we've lived here ever since [pause] the kids grew up in South Pas. And I was on the desegregation committee task force at the school there, and I saw the school go from 30 percent minority to 66 percent in a period of three years. I think it's been negative in that a lot of the people that have come over have been, well, like the

Vietnamese family was from the country and not educated. They don't assimilate well. I think it's negative on the whole.

Clearly, their own conditional status has heightened their intolerance toward others who might upset the delicate balance. Even respondents who recognize the fallacy of judging Asian immigrants so harshly find it difficult to refrain. Marie Nishida, for instance, acknowledged that her own ancestors were probably viewed as problematically as current immigrants. Nevertheless, she could not deny her own prejudices toward them:

Q: Does their presence affect your life in any way?

A: Yeah, brings up a lot of feelings you have to deal with [laugh]. I mean, as a native Californian, I guess it's like you can understand how a lot of the American-born Asians feel towards immigrants. I don't think it's right because all they have to do is look back a couple generations, and it's the same thing. But at the same time it's like, "God damn, who do these guys think they are? They come out with their Mercedes Benzes and all this money." But that's not all of them, but those ones stick out, they kinda I guess, get the eye of your native, so-called native Californians. It's interesting. Definitely interesting.

Patti Ito also acknowledged how immigrants are unfairly blamed for the actions of others, namely "white people," who disregard cultural differences between Asian immigrants and ethnics. Even with this understanding, however, she too felt the tug of resentment:

[J]ust because the cultures are different, people view them as different and all these stereotypes like they're bad drivers. And there's just a whole bunch of stereotypes against them, and I don't really know why, but it gives us Asian-Americans a bad name because other people, a lot of white people just clump us all together because they don't realize there's a big cultural difference between the immigrants and the Asian-Americans. And I think that's kind of disappointing because I think it makes us as Asian-Americans not too receptive to the immigrants, and I just think it creates more barriers.

In their eagerness to prove to themselves and others that they are "real" Americans then, our respondents end up being the least tolerant of immigrants who cast a shadow over their Americanness. The cost is simply too high and their status simply too precarious to warrant much sympathy for them.

▦ *Summary*

As racialized ethnics, our respondents maneuver between a maze of choices and constraints in constructing an identity for themselves. On one hand they feel constrained to identify in ethnic or racial terms because others continue to define, respond to, and treat them as separate from the American mainstream. Despite their long-standing roots in this country, they understand that others still view them as foreigners and therefore may approach them with curiosity ("I've been to China before" "Where did you learn to speak English so well?" "Tell me about Chinese culture") or hostility ("Go back to your country!" "Stop stealing our jobs"). As such, identifying solely as an American, they believe, is not an option available to them as yet.

On the other hand, there are signs of resistance and reappropriation as they struggle to work within imposed limitations and fashion an identity that resonates for them. As such, many insist on a hyphenated identity in order to honor their American as well as ethnic roots. The sentiment, "I may be Chinese, but I'm an American too," captures this spirit. Furthermore, as ethnic distinctions matter less and less in the face of an emerging racial consciousness, they are increasingly embracing an Asian-American identity (Espiritu, 1992; Onishi, 1996).

Conclusion ▣ CHAPTER 7
The Racialized Ethnic Experience

Interest in O. J. Simpson has long since waned; both trials, criminal and civil, have come and gone. Similarly, Judge Ito has faded from the limelight and into the Who's Who annals of obscure American history ("For 100 points name me the judge in the Simpson trial"). The conclusion to the Simpson cases marked the closing of a disappointing chapter for Asian-Americans. Initially, Asian-Americans met news of Ito's appointment with enthusiasm because the media rarely portrays Asian-Americans, and when it does, their bias toward caricatured representations of foreigners speaking in broken English is clear. Therefore, the role Ito would play in the "media event of the century" pleased them. In him Asian-Americans had a confident and articulate representative. Not only Japanese-Americans but many Asian-Americans overall felt great pride in knowing that, at last, one of their own would occupy a position of international prominence and respect.

However, as criticism mounted against the judge's handling of the case, anxiety replaced pride. Would Ito's performance reflect poorly on Asian-Americans as a whole? Would his inability to control attorneys on both sides confirm stereotypes that Asians were not assertive? They understood all too well that more was riding on the judge's performance than strictly his individual reputation; by extension, all Asian-Americans stood to be judged by his performance. Senator D'Amato's antics only confirmed their concerns by reinforcing a stereotype Asian ethnics have fought against all their lives.

More recently, another public spectacle grabbed the attention of Asian-Americans, the Senate hearings into alleged campaign fund-raising abuses. Again, they watched closely because more was riding on the hearings than the individual fates of former Democratic National Committee (D.N.C.) fund-raiser John Huang, Little Rock restaurateur Charlie (Yah Lin) Trie, and other Asians and Asian-Americans suspected of funneling illegal foreign contributions.

Of course, allegations of an "invasion" by foreign Asian sources trying to buy influence among American politicians play off an old theme. That the possible wrongdoing of a handful of Asians and Asian-Americans can cast a shadow over all Asian-American donors is an all-too-familiar scenario. Contributors with the misfortune of having an Asian or Asian-sounding last name had to endure intrusive questions concerning their citizenship status, annual income, who employs them, and requests for credit checks to verify their source of income. As Daphne Kwok, executive director for the Organization of Chinese Americans, put it, "Wouldn't a more neutral approach be to investigate all contributions over $5,000 and not just those targeting the A.P.A. [Asian Pacific American] community?" (Elsner, 1997)

The worst abuses to come out of the scandal have, not surprisingly, played up on the "foreignness" of those involved, a point aptly captured by Senator Daniel Akaka during a speech delivered to the Senate on March 20, 1997:

> Clearly, in some quarters, "Asian" and "Asian-American" are synonymous, unlike the case with Europeans and European-Americans. In fact, the term "European" Americans is rarely heard in public discourse, because the ethnic origin of European Americans is not presumed to have a bearing on their patriotism. ("From the Senate," 1997, p. 7)

In typical D'Amato fashion, Kansas Senator Sam Brownback couldn't resist a pidgen-inflected barb concerning Huang's fund-raising activities during the Senate hearings: "*No raise money, no get bonus.*" Similarly, Georgia Representative Jack Kingston let out the quip that illegal donations were only the "tip of the egg roll." That both men felt free enough from recrimination to engage in such racist witticisms speaks volumes about the atmosphere during the hearings.

Perhaps the worst example of foreign caricature to emerge from the campaign scandal involved the March 24, 1997, cover illustration for the conservative magazine *National Review*. The cover depicted President Clinton wearing a coolie outfit (baggy jacket and pants, straw hat, slippers, hair queue) and serving tea; Hillary Clinton in a Chairman Mao uniform (complete with little red book); and Vice President Al Gore in a Buddhist monk's robe. Both the president and first lady had exaggerated buck teeth and slanted eyes. In a bizarre twist of events, however, the *National Review* claimed to be victimized. Responding to Asian-American leaders' demands for an apology, editor John O'Sullivan not only dismissed their demands but claimed that "people in the ethnic grievance game" were unfairly targeting his magazine and him; the *National Review*, he claimed, was owed an apology, not the other way around (Wu, F., 1997).

▨ I opened this book with a detailed discussion of the Ito-D'Amato incident and I return to it now, along with an overview of the current campaign finance scandal, because both situations capture two of the most meaningful findings to come out of this study. First, not only is racism still an issue haunting middle-class Asian ethnics, the particular strain that plagues them also involves xenophobic elements that play up the notion of being foreign. Their class status has done little to validate their authenticity as long-time Americans in the eyes of the public. Second, the fate of individual Asian ethnics is still inextricably tied to that of other Asian-Americans and Asian nationals. The campaign finance scandal speaks particularly well to this point. How Asian and Asian-American contributions came to be singled out and why whipping up anxiety among the American public was so easy speaks directly to the unique way in which they are marked off and made "other." Whether native-born or immigrant, Asian-Americans remain what Lowe (1996) calls the "foreigner-within."

To be sure, the Asian ethnics we spoke with are not obsessed with figuring out how their racialized ethnic identities play out in their daily lives. For the most part, they do not ponder daily over what it means to be Asian-American, Chinese-American, or Japanese-American; most keep busy with the demands of work and family. Consistently enough, however, our respondents are reminded of their conditional status in this society and that financial success does not guarantee social acceptability. The public continues to resist embracing Asian-Americans *en masse* as one of "us"; while individuals may gain acceptance within their immediate social circles, the larger group boundary remains firm (Alba, 1985).

▨ Features of the Asian Ethnic Experience

From my examination of the Asian ethnic experience, four key characteristics that convey how their lives converge and diverge from the white ethnic experience emerge. Each is listed below and followed by a detailed discussion:

1. Asian ethnics exercise a great deal of flexibility regarding the cultural elements they wish to keep or discard from *their personal lives*. What they have retained by way of cultural traditions is largely symbolic and a novelty.
2. How they choose to identify, however, is not a private affair. They experience pressure to identify in ethnic or racial terms because these remain salient markers to others.
3. Despite their generational longevity in this country, an assumption of foreignness stubbornly clings to them.
4. Asian ethnics are not considered "real" Americans. They have not been incorporated into the collective memory of who qualifies as a "real" American.

Symbolic Ethnicity and Asian Ethnics

As third-generation and later Americans, Asian ethnics are highly attuned to the cultural styles and values of the white, middle-class American mainstream; they have not retained much by way of Chinese or Japanese cultural traditions. What little they do about traditional activities is carried out, at most, a few times a year and without much reverence. Similar to the white ethnics studied by Alba (1990), Waters (1990), and others (Bershtel & Graubard, 1992; Crispino, 1980; Kellogg, 1990; Lieberson, 1985), our respondents are flexible regarding the cultural elements they wish to integrate or discard from their *personal lives*. They experience few qualms with creatively reinterpreting or discarding cultural elements they find incongruent with their lifestyle. In this sense, Gans's (1979) notion of symbolic ethnicity is useful for describing the state of their cultural observance. Our respondents are more concerned with expressing an ethnic identity than with maintaining traditional cultural practices. Furthermore, they feel free to choose those aspects of Chinese or Japanese culture that fit into their lifestyle and discard what does not.

Ethnic Expectations

Nevertheless, Asian ethnics face societal expectations to *be ethnic* since others assume they should be closer to their ethnic roots than to their American ones. Whereas for later generation white ethnics to identify along ethnic lines is a matter of personal choice, our respondents have not found this to be the case for them; not identifying in ethnic or racial terms is problematic in their interactions with non-Asians. In this sense, Asian ethnics are not free to be symbolically ethnic to the extent that white ethnics are. Symbolic ethnicity for the latter, as Steinberg (1989) argues, comes out of a crisis of cultural authenticity that has left later generations with only high profile symbols to champion: "People desperately wish to 'feel' ethnic precisely because they have all but lost the prerequisites of 'being' ethnic" (p. 63). Asian ethnics, on the other hand, are expected to "be ethnic" in spite of the same loss of cultural authenticity accompanying extensive acculturation. Others consistently expect them to identify ethnically (e.g., as Chinese or Japanese) or racially as Asian and be knowledgeable about Chinese or Japanese "things" and to express dissatisfaction when they are not. Questions such as "Where are you *really* from?" and "What are you?" convey the message that they are not seen as legitimate members of this society despite their long history (Ancheta, 1998).

From comments such as these and other cues (stereotyping, intentional prejudice, discrimination, etc.), they have learned that their racial and ethnic background remain salient markers to others and influence how they are defined, responded to, and treated. How they choose to live their lives may be a private affair, how they publicly identify clearly is not. They must deal with others' expectations and an imposed racialized ethnic identity despite their generally loose ties to traditional cultural patterns.

"American Beats Kwan" Revisited: The Foreigner Image

At the root of these expectations lies a deeply held assumption that all Asians in this country are newcomers. Despite a collective history spanning more than 150 years, Asian ethnics still face stubborn resistance and incredulity when they attempt to assert their third-generation or later American status. Some non-Asians respond with shock or bewilderment over this news, shaking their heads in disbelief that Asians have been around as long as or longer than they have.

I would like to return for a moment to an incident first introduced in Chapter 2. MSNBC's gaffe over the women's Olympic figure skating championships ("American Beats Kwan") captures just how deep the foreigner stereotype runs. By normalizing Tara Lipinski as the American and "othering" Michelle Kwan, MSNBC was guilty merely of getting caught—what they printed simply reflected what many others believe to be true, that Americans look like Tara while foreigners look like Michelle.

Six years earlier, Kristi Yamaguchi, the 1992 gold medal winner in women's figure skating, also faced difficulty in being seen as one of America's own. While winning the gold brought immediate fame and fortune for Peggy Fleming and Dorothy Hamill, Kristi had trouble trying to cash in on her gold medal (Magiera, 1992; Swift, 1992; Zinn, 1992). In accounting for why she was not being flooded with requests for product endorsements, Magiera (1992) writes:

[Kristi] Yamaguchi has not signed any new contracts since her Olympic victory, raising speculation that her Japanese-American heritage is hindering efforts on the part of International Management Group to bill her as the quintessential "California Girl." (p. 10)

My personal favorite account for why Kristi did not fare as well as her predecessors comes not from the academic but the pop world. Tabloid staple *People Magazine* perhaps summarized it best by stating:

> Kristi Yamaguchi may have won the Olympic gold last year, but bronze medal–winner Nancy Kerrigan got the gasps for her Grace Kelly gleam. Called by the Boston Globe "America's ice queen and poster girl," (just check out her six-figure endorsements), the 5–foot 4–inch Kerrigan, 23, will acknowledge only one secret about her beauty. "Short skirts make you look taller." Pal Paul Wylie, though, an Olympic Silver medalist, cuts right to her charm: "Nancy's the girl next door." ("The 50 Most Beautiful," 1998)

Apparently for Kristi, being the girl next door from Fremont, a Bay Area bedroom community, does not count. Or is it that she doesn't have that Grace Kelly (read: white) gleam?

To be sure, a major reason underlying this assumption of foreignness stems from contemporary Asian immigration. The influx of unprecedented numbers of immigrants has complicated the lives of native-born Asian ethnics because most non-Asians are unable or unwilling to recognize generational differences. Their high visibility and concentration in a handful of states has magnified the intensity of their presence, leading to the incorrect assumption that all Asians are newcomers. Even in states without significant Asian representation, however, the presumption is that all Asians must be recent arrivals since media portrayals focus primarily on the foreign-born. The average television viewer has not been offered prolonged exposure to Asians who do not have an accent or who are not presented as exotic.

Because of the impressive number of Asian immigrants arriving and their high visibility, the question naturally arises whether the stamp of foreignness plaguing Asian ethnics would disappear if immigration were curtailed or if their entry had continued to

Doonesbury   BY GARRY TRUDEAU

FIGURE 7.1. Doonesbury Cartoon. Doonesbury © 1996 G. B. Trudeau. Reprinted with permission of Universal Press Syndicate. All rights reserved.

be denied. Perhaps within a few generations Asian ethnics would, as European ethnics before them, gradually be absorbed into the American mainstream. My sense, however, is that Asian ethnics would still be marginalized even without contemporary immigration. The arrival on the scene of immigrants has only helped to cement foreignness as a metaphor to distance them from the general population.

Furthermore, I am skeptical that within a few generations Asian-Americans would *automatically* be absorbed into the mainstream. Generations of highly acculturated Asian ethnics who speak without an accent have lived in this country, and yet most white Americans have not heard of or ever really seen them. They are America's invisible citizenry, the accountants who do our taxes, engineers who safeguard our infrastructure, and pharmacists who fill our prescriptions. Nevertheless, over the years they have continued to be treated and seen as other.

Who Is an American?

It would only be a slight exaggeration to say that the quintessential American experience is rooted in the experience of immigration. The ability to recall an earlier time when one's ancestors traveled great and unfamiliar distances to seek a new life, the difficulties they faced, their eventual triumph over adversity, and their contributions toward building a new nation are the stuff from which we have built our cultural mythology—countless American morality tales have been written using this basic template. White ethnics today are united by this collective public memory—the journey across the Atlantic and subsequent pioneer experience are recalled nostalgically as rites of passage toward becoming an American (Alba, 1990; Bodnar, 1992).

I remember as a child watching Saturday morning cartoons and singing along to the Schoolhouse Rock series of informational cartoons—they provided mini lessons in history, civics, and learning the ABC's. One of the most memorable to me was the one with the theme, "Great American Melting Pot," replete with giant stew pot and little people walking up a plank in their traditional garb on one side and coming out as little patriots on the other. Countless children grew up watching that cartoon and believing in the lessons it had to offer. And yet, crucial pieces of information were missing from that sweet image. The fact that African-Americans were forcibly brought over on slave ships or that Native-Americans and Mexicans were forcibly incorporated against their will adds a troubling element to an otherwise straightforward picture of assimilation. Nor let us forget the 1790 Naturalization Act that restricted citizenship eligibility to "free white persons," and that was not fully nullified until 1952. In other words, while all the little people from around the world may have walked up that plank, only some were allowed to jump into the stew; hidden from view was the little door on the side where countless generations of non-Europeans were ushered through and pushed back down into the masses.

So whatever became of all those people who were rejected from the stew? If their experiences do not neatly fit with the collective memory of what it took to become an American, where does that leave them today? For Asian ethnics, it leaves them feeling like "guests in someone else's house," as Ron Wakabayashi so eloquently put it, unable to relax and really get comfortable (see Chapter 1 for the complete quote). Not only do they not fit the romanticized and sentimentalized account of assimilation offered in the melting pot metaphor, their own pioneer roots, unique experiences, and contributions in building this country have been and continue to be erased from collective memory. Lowe (1996) speaks powerfully to this point in her work on the Asian-American experience as she explains how and why Asian-Americans continue to be outside the cultural and racial boundaries of the nation. As Alba (1990) argues, what it means to be an American continues to demand European ancestry. Whites continue to feel a sense of "proprietary claim" to being the "real" Americans (Blumer, 1958).

Today, Asian ethnics exercise a great deal of personal choice regarding the elements of traditional ethnic culture they wish to incorporate or do away with. For the most part being Chinese-American or Japanese-American is not preeminent in their minds. They befriend whom they please, date and marry whom they please, choose the careers they please, and pursue further knowledge about their cultural heritage if they please. In this sense, ethnicity has indeed become optional in our respondents' personal lives. But in another very real way, being ethnic remains a societal expectation for them. They have yet to be embraced as bona fide longtime Americans and to be accepted as the highly acculturated Americans they are. The pain and frustration accompanying this exclusion are captured in the following statement by Carol Wong, a third-generation Chinese-American and dietician:

> I had just moved to New York, maybe four months, and this doctor came up to me and said something to me in Chinese, and I turned around and said something like "Are you talking to me?" And he said yeah, and I said, "I don't speak Chinese." This was a Caucasian guy . . . and he starts going into this tirade like, "Are you ashamed of where you came from da da da da." And I turned around to him, and I looked him straight in the face, and I said, "How many Americans do you know who go around speaking Chinese? I'm not ashamed of where I come from. I come from Fresno. The place that provides you with those little red boxes of Sun-Maid Raisins."

In subtle and not so subtle ways, Asian ethnics continue to find themselves excluded from the racial and cultural center, to be denied their rightful sense of place in this nation. Although longtime Americans, they fail to be perceived as such. Instead, they remain "model minorities," the best of the "other" bunch but not "real" Americans.

▨ *Personal Costs Borne by Asian Ethnics*

Asian ethnics pay numerous personal costs as a consequence of their conditional status, costs that are conveniently denied beneath the glowing image of the "model minority." First and foremost, they expend emotional and mental energy keeping their social "antennae" out to assess how safe their social surroundings are.

I am reminded here of Paul Leong's reflections on how always being alert to possible racial tensions has "socially hindered" him. The fear, irrational or not, that somebody might physically harm them or that international tensions between the United States and China or Japan might have repercussions in their own lives costs them their sense of well-being. That so many of our respondents feel vulnerable in this regard is a particularly disturbing finding and one that parallels findings drawn from work on the black middle class. Many spoke of the psychological exhaustion and wasted time and energy spent worrying about things that whites need not think about because they have the privilege not to. Energy is also expended trying to recover from internalized negative stereotypes and building up damaged self-esteem.

There are also significant costs paid in the form of intolerance toward Asian immigrants. It is an irony that many of our respondents, in their quest to gain recognition for being legitimate Americans, they become the quintessential "ugly Americans," nativists who resent and look down upon immigrants. Sadly, there is little room for tolerance when one's own status is precarious. Lee's (1997) work with Asian-American youth found similar examples of arrogance and intolerance being directed across ethnic lines.

Another cost which I have not yet touched upon but is related to the last point concerns the intolerance and racism some of our respondents direct toward other racial minority groups and the reasons for their intolerance. While everyone acknowledges that a racial hierarchy exists with whites at the top, not everyone responds to this realization in the same way. Those with seek to challenge the hierarchy are more likely to politicize their racial identity and, therefore, embrace alliances with other racially subordinated groups. Tracy Nagata, for example, spoke of the camaraderie she believes exists between "people of color" as oppressed peoples, and Andy Kawachi referred to the need for "blacks, Latinos, and Asians to stick together to fight the good fight rather than fighting amongst ourselves."

Those whose interests have less to do with dismantling racist structures and more with gaining acceptance, on the other hand, are more likely to adopt the 110 percent American outlook discussed by Nagata (1993) in Chapter 3. Like the Korean and Asian-identified students in Lee's (1996) study, they hold out hope that Asian-Americans might eventually be able to "put their feet up on the table" and be seen as legitimate Americans. As a result, their strategy is to prove to whites how worthy they are of being welcomed into the fold by embracing the model minority stereotype. Instead of becoming disillusioned, they adopt the attitude "if I just try harder. . . . " A consequence of embracing this outlook, however, is that other racial groups who do not pull themselves "up by their own bootstraps" by expecting government assistance in the form of affirmative action programs or who complain about racism are seen as whiners and troublemakers. In their own efforts to gain acceptance then, they end up denying the systemic nature of racial inequality despite seeing how it has operated in their own lives and their families.

Forever Foreigners or Honorary Whites?

The time has come to more directly deal with the question posed by the title of this book along with an unstated but implied accompanying question. Are Asian ethnics "forever foreigners" or "honorary whites," and as Okihiro (1994) and Ancheta (1998) ask, is yellow black or white? Of course, the short answer to both questions is no since these dualisms defy the complex nature of race relations operating in this society. For example, calling them forever foreigners denies the ways Asian ethnics are advantaged compared to other racial groups by virtue of their model minority designation and the impact this has on interminority relations. Conversely, calling them honorary whites denies the unique combination of nativism and racism they experience and the myriad ways they continue to be marginalized by the racial and cultural center. And as far as the black-white question goes, Ancheta (1998) provides one of the best summary statements I have seen:

In essence a black-white model fails to recognize that the basic nature of discrimination can differ among racial and ethnic groups. Theories of racial inferiority have been applied, often with violent force, against Asian-Americans, just as they have been applied against blacks and other racial minority groups. But the causes of anti-Asian subordination can be traced to other factors as well, including nativism, differences in language and culture, perceptions of Asians as economic competitors, international relations, and past military involvement in Asian countries. . . . All of these considerations point to the need for an analysis of race that is very different from the dominant black-white paradigm. (p. 13)

To repeat, then, yellow is neither black nor white, and Asian ethnics are neither outcasts nor honorary members of the inner circle who have been invited to take their shoes off and get comfortable. Their experiences stand on their own and must be assessed based on criteria unique to their circumstances.

The Shifting Nature and Meaning of Ethnicity

[I]f plural cultures are to be maintained, they must be carried on by subsocieties which provide the framework for communal existence—their own networks of cliques, institutions, organizations, and informal friendship patterns—functioning not only for the first generation of immigrants but for the succeeding generation of American-born descendants as well. And here a crucial theoretical point must be recognized. While it is not possible for cultural pluralism to exist without the existence of separate subsocieties, the reverse is not the case. It *is* possible for separate subsocieties to continue their existence even while the cultural differences between them become progressively reduced and even in greater part eliminated. (Gordon, 1964, p. 158)

As in previous studies of later generation Americans, my findings confirm the declining significance of old ethnic cultures. Most of our respondents have quite modern views concerning the role ethnic traditions should play in their lives. I am reminded here of the insights offered earlier by Greg Okinaka: "The Japan that my parents knew when they were my age was a completely different Japan than I know at my current age. And it's gonna be a different Japan that any other generations learn fifteen or twenty years from now."

In the midst of such contemporary views, however, I have also found evidence of strong communal ties combined with a high value placed on ethnic and, increasingly, panethnic, association. Clearly, not everyone embraces this value, but certainly more do so than would be expected given their generational status (Fugita & O'Brien, 1991a). The activities they engage in with their Asian-American friends, however, would hardly qualify as ethnic by any traditional criteria. Asian-American volleyball and other sport leagues, Christian churches, and professional business associations are only some of the activities our respondents define as ethnic activities. While some might question just "how ethnic" these activities really are, our respondents have no trouble identifying them as such since they were raised to believe that activities shared with other Asian-Americans or coethnics constitute ethnic activities.

Such an attitude has serious implications for the study of contemporary ethnic life since it raises the need to consider whether fellowship is enough to sustain a distinct ethnic identity. Gordon (1964) certainly thought so; as captured in the passage above, he believed ethnic groups could successfully maintain separate identities and structurally parallel institutions indefinitely. That is, members of ethnic groups could lead highly acculturated lifestyles but do so with other ethnic members. Steinberg (1989), in contrast, questions whether ethnic communities can maintain themselves after losing their cultural distinctiveness. He asks, "Can ethnic communities maintain their boundaries at the same time that their cultures are eroding from within?" (p. 67).

My position on this matter leans in Gordon's (1964) direction. There is little social or psychological cost, as far as many of our respondents are concerned, with participating in such organizations and institutions. In fact, they join them precisely because they are enjoyable and comforting experiences. Furthermore, they believe they are contributing toward building an emergent culture and reaffirming their membership in this constituency.

The future of contemporary ethnic life may not look very different from contemporary mainstream cultural patterns. What, after all, is the difference between an Asian-American volleyball league and an ethnically nonspecific one? The answer is probably not much in terms of the level of sweat expended or the rules governing play. What is different is the intent involved in coming together. Those who join ethnic clubs and organizations are consciously choosing to do so because they place value on associating with others like themselves based on the perception of common upbringing and even experiences with marginalization. How stable can such a basis for community be depends on a number of variables. As Gordon (1964) argues, these outlets exist in part because of the prejudices of the majority and in part by the desire of the groups to maintain their own communal identity and subculture. So long as they find them enjoyable and necessary, they will continue to exist.

▣ *Embracing a Panethnic or Racialized Identity*

The ease with which our respondents are broadening their boundaries of group inclusiveness and embracing a panethnic identity further lends strong support to scholars studying panethnic formations (Espiritu, 1992; Nagel, 1994, 1995; Shinagawa & Pang, 1996). Ethnic divisions that once stood firm are clearly blurring among the later generations; marriages between different Asian ethnic groups, for instance, that would have been socially frowned upon only a generation ago are now commonplace.

Their openness to dating other Asian-Americans is both cause and effect of the intense boundary shift that is taking place as Asian ethnics are coming to embrace a racialized and panethnic identity. Especially as distinct cultural patterns continue to be watered down and replaced by a more generalized Asian-American culture, individuals are less likely to focus on ethnic differences and instead, recognize the similarities linking their experiences. Importantly, those similarities are grounded in their common experience of being viewed and treated as a distinct racial group in the United States. While the impetus for this boundary expansion may not have originated from group members, the resulting identity has taken on a life and meaning of its own as those members have taken to constructing a cultural base reflecting their common experiences.

In Conclusion

Will we be able, decades from now, to look back at the current experiences of Asian ethnics as but a rite of passage, a period of momentary social exclusion experienced by virtually all groups as they enter the final stages in the assimilation process? It may be that Asian ethnics are on the road to attaining full social acceptance and that the current influx of Asian immigrants has merely complicated the picture temporarily. From a wider lens of time, we might indeed find that Asian ethnics are entering that "twilight" period of their ethnicity as discussed by Alba (1985) regarding Italian-Americans today.

There are other reasons for optimism. Some of our respondents are themselves optimistic that someday Asian-Americans may be seen as legitimate members of this society. Some believe this will have to happen through political activism and struggle on the part of Asian-Americans to demand recognition of their contributions and place in society. Others have greater hope in the American system and believe that democratic principles of fairness and inclusiveness will win out in the end. They point to the lessening of discrimination that has occurred since their parents' generation.

Virtually all believe, however, that large-scale social inclusion will not take place in their lifetimes. More likely, if it happens at all it will be their children or grandchildren who might finally feel a sense of security over their place in this society. In the meantime, they continue to live productive lives and enjoy many of the fruits society has to offer. The one fruit that remains out of their reach, however, is peace of mind. The sense that "it can all be taken away" continues to haunt many even as they hope for the best in the future.

APPENDIX A

INTERVIEW QUESTIONNAIRE

Name:
Age:
Generation:

1. Early Experiences

To start, please tell me about the place or places where you grew up:

- Is this where were you born?
- What kind of people lived in your neighborhood?
- Who were your playmates?

How about the schools (K-12) you attended. Would you describe them for me:

- What kind of people did you go to school with?
    - What were the ethnicities of your closest friends?
    - (If Asians were present) did you seek them out? Why/why not?
    - Do you think you had a preference?

Do you remember ever experiencing any racism or discrimination when you were growing up?

- What happened?

- Where?
- Can you describe to me how that made you feel?

Did you have much contact with other Chinese/Japanese?

- Where did this happen?

When you were growing up, how conscious do you think you were of being Chinese/Japanese?
Where is it that you went to college?

- Tell me about your closest friends (where met, ethnicity, still in contact, etc.)

Some people say that college is a time for exploring one's ethnic identity.

- Would you say that this was true for you?
  - (if yes) What do you think motivated your interest?
- Was this a sudden interest or had it been there all along?
- Did you take any Asian-American studies or Asian history courses?
- Did you study an Asian language?
- Were you a member of any ethnic clubs?

2. Family Influences

Now I'd like to ask you some questions about your family and family history:

- Who in your family were the original immigrants?
  - Where did they come from?
  - How long ago did they come here?
  - Where did they settle?
  - What did they do for work?
  - How do you know this information?

And your family now, where are they all located? (parents, siblings, grandparents)

- What do they do for work?

Now I'd like you to think about your family and what they were like when you were growing up:

- Thinking back to your memories of your father, did you think of him as being particularly Chinese/Japanese or particularly American or a combination?
- (Repeat question for mother)
- How important do you think it was to your parents that you be familiar with Chinese/Japanese culture?
- Any aspects in particular?
- How did they express this to you?
- What kinds of cultural information or practices did they teach you?
- Was Chinese/Japanese ever spoken at home?
  - By whom?
- How often did you see your grandparents?
  - Mother's side and father's side?
  - Did you have a close relationship?
  - Did they teach you about Chinese/Japanese culture?
  - Are your grandparents still alive?
  - How often do you see them now?
- How often would you say your family ate Chinese/Japanese meals?
  - Did your parents prepare these meals, or did you go to restaurants?
  - Did you eat these meals, or did your parents prepare something else for you?
- Did your family celebrate any Chinese/Japanese holidays?
  - Which one(s)?
- Did your family ever talk to you about racism or discrimination?
- (for Japanese ethnics only) Did any member of your family ever talk to you about the Japanese internment experience?
  - How much do you know about Japanese internment?

- How do you know this information?

3. Current Lifestyle and Ethnic Practices

Now I'd like to ask you some questions about your life now:

- Where do you work?
    - Are there any other Asians at work?
    - Do you have much contact with any of them?
    - Outside of work, how much contact do you have with other Chinese/Japanese or Asians?
- How often would you say you eat Chinese/Japanese food nowadays?
    - Do you prepare it yourself or do you go to a restaurant?
- Do you celebrate any Chinese/Japanese holidays?
    - Which ones?
    - How do you celebrate?
    - With whom do you celebrate?
- Can you speak or read Chinese/Japanese?
    - Where and when did you learn?
    - Whom do you speak Chinese/Japanese with?

How knowledgable would you say you are about Chinese/Japanese history and culture?

- Have you ever been to Japan/China?
    - When?
    - What were your motivations for going?
    - (if not) Do you have any interest in going?
- What are the ethnicities of your closest friends?
    - Where met?
    - Do you have any Chinese/Japanese/Asian American friends?
- Do you belong to any ethnic clubs or organizations?
    - Why did you decide to join?
- Have you ever been involved in an interracial relationship? (probe)
    - How many of your previous relationships have been interracial?

- Do you have a preference one way or the other?
- How often do/have you date(ed) interracially?
  - Are you married now or currently in a relationship?
    - What is the ethnicity of your spouse/mate?
      (For Intermarried:)
      - How did you meet your husband/wife?
      - How often, if ever, does your being Chinese/Japanese come up in your relationship?
      - Was it an issue for your respective families that you chose each other?
      - In your opinion are intermarried couples any different from couples who are not intermarried?
        - Do they face any additional issues?
      - Have you ever noticed people staring at you and your spouse because you are an interracial couple?
    - In what ways, if any, is the life you have created with your spose particularly Chinese/Japanese?
    - Do you have children or plan to have children?
    - How important is it to you that your children know about Japanese/Chinese roots?
    - What will you do to accomplish this?
    - Has anybody else in your family intermarried?
      (for respondents currently involved in interracial relationship):
        - Is this your first interracial relationship?
        - How did you meet?
        - Do your parents have a preference one way or the other for you to marry/date other Chinese/Japanese?

4. *Ethnic Identity Issues*

Now I'd like to ask you some questions about the ways in which you think about yourself:

- Would you describe yourself an Chinese-American/Japanese-American, American, Asian-American, Asian,

Chinese/Japanese, or what?

- What does that mean to you, to consider yourself XXXX?
- Would you describe for me how being Chinese/Japanese is different from being American, if at all?
- (if respondent did not answer "American") Would you ever consider calling yourself an "American" plain and simple?
- How do you think your parents see you, as more Chinese/Japanese or more American?
    - (repeat for spouse/mate)
    - (repeat for people at work)
    - (repeat for closest friends)
    - (if different, for all 3, ask why)
- Can you think of any specific times in your life that being Chinese/Japanese has been more or less important to you?

Immigrants from Asia currently make up one of the largest incoming groups into California.

- Do you think their presence affects the lives of people like yourself who have lived here for many generations, in any way?
- How about your life in particular?
- How much contact if any do you have with Asian immigrants?
- Do you have any friends who are Asian immigrants?
- Do you feel that most Americans are able to tell the difference between Chinese/Japanese immigrants and Americans of Chinese/Japanese ancestry?
- Do you think most Americans can tell the difference between different Asian groups overall?
- Have you ever been mistaken for a Chinese/Japanese/Korean/etc.?
- Have you ever been mistaken for an immigrant?
    - By whom?
    - How did it make you feel?
- Has anybody ever said to you, "your English is good"?

- What was your response?
- How did that make you feel?
- Has anybody ever asked you "where are you from," meaning to ask "what is your ethnicity"?
- Do you think this is a question European ethnics are ever asked?

Occasionally, newspapers or television will run stories on Asian Americans.

- To what degree do you feel any sense of personal connection with the Asian Americans in the story?
- In general, would you say you feel any special kinship to other Asians?

5. Societal Perceptions and Influences

Now I'd like to ask you some questions about how other people see you:

- How often do people ask or comment on your racial or ethnic background?
- How do you typically respond?
- How do you generally feel when people ask/comment?
- Have you ever felt out of place or uncomfortable because you are Chinese/Japanese? (probe)
- Has anybody ever made assumptions about you based on larger stereotypes about Chinese/Japanese?
- Do you ever feel any social pressure to have a strong ethnic background/identity?
- Do you believe there is racial discrimination in the U.S.?
    - Who are the victims of racial discrimination?
- In the past, Asian-Americans were subjected to significant amounts of discrimination.
    - In your opinion, do they still experience discrimination today?
    - In your opinion, do they experience more/less/same amount as blacks? Latinos? whites?
- As an adult, have you ever experienced what you

believe to be racism or prejudice?

- ■ What happened?
- ■ How often does this occur?
- ■ How do you typically respond?

■ Do you know of other Asian-Americans who have experienced what they believed to be discrimination or prejudice?

■ Have you ever personally ever felt that being a Chinese/Japanese was a handicap to fully participating in American society?

■ When you have traveled in the past, have you ever felt out of place because you are a Chinese/Japanese?

- ■ Where did you feel this?
- ■ What made you feel like this?

■ If the U.S. were to go to war right now with Japan/China or any other part of Asia, do you feel that the way people perceive you might change?

- ■ How about if the U.S. went to war with Italy, Germany, etc. would the lives of Italian-Americans, etc. change?

■ Do you feel that something like Japanese Internment could happen again?

■ Do you think it means something different to say that you're an American of Irish descent compared to saying you're an American of Japanese/Chinese descent?

APPENDIX B

LIST OF RESPONDENTS

Name	Age Category	Marital Status	Occupation	Family Relation
1. Pete Takezawa	mid 40s	single	writer	
2. Jonathan Tse	mid 20s	single	business owner	
3. Marie Nishida	late 40s	married (Chinese)	clerical	
4. Paul Leong	late 20s	married (Filipina)	graduate student	
5. Rick Lew	mid 20s	single	graduate student	brother of #6; son of #7
6. Eve Lew	mid 30s	single	therapist/ social worker	sister of #5; daughter of #7
7. Wilma Lew	late 50s	married	business owner	mother of #5 and #6
8. Sharon Young	mid 20s	single	veterinary technician	
9. Jerry Fong	early 20s	single	student	
10. Kevin Fong	mid 20s	single	construction finance	
11. Winston Jung	late 50s	married	professor (retired)	
12. Arne Kumamoto	early 30s	married	administrator	
13. Ron Kita	early 20s	single	administrator	
14. Tony Lam**	late 40s	single	teacher	
15. Roberta Huang	early 50s	widowed	business owner	
16. Theresa Ikuta	early 20s	single	lab technician	
17. Meg Takahashi	late 30s	single	library assistant	
18. Bret Higashi	mid 20s	single	medical student	
19. Frank Wu	early 50s	married	scientist and engineer	

Name	Age Category	Marital Status	Occupation	Family Relation
20. Morrison Hum	mid 60s	married	school principal (retired)	
21. Shirley Hum	early 60s	married	school nurse (retired)	spouse of #20
22. Karen Murakami	early 30s	married (Japanese)	nutritionist	daughter of #20
23. Elise Lim	late 20s	engaged	statistician	engaged to #24
24. Andrew Lee	late 20s	engaged	statistician	engaged to #23
25. Peter Gong	mid 70s (white)	married	commercial artist (retired)	
26. Gary Hong	early 20s	single	law student	
27. Lonnie Wong	early 20s	single	student	
28. Emily Woo**	mid 20s	single	nonprofit organizer	
29. Chris Takeuchi	late 40s	married	museum curator	
30. Peggy Endo	early 50s	married	corporate administrator	
31. Jan Muramoto	late 30s	married	homemaker	
32. Eileen Inouye	late 20s	married	social worker	
33. Darlene Lee	early 20s	single	pharmacy student	
34. Amy Matsuyama	late 40s	single	clerical	
35. Greg Okinaka	early 20s	single	financial consultant	
36. Rick Wubara	late 20s	single	journalist	
37. David Ito	mid 40s	married	real estate	spouse of #38; father of 40; brother of 39
38. Lorraine Ito	mid 40s	married	accountant	spouse of #37; mother of 40
39. Carl Ito	mid 30s	married (Filipina)	pharmacist	brother of #37
40. Patti Ito	mid 20s	single	optometry student	daughter of #37
41. Daphne Kitano	mid 20s	single	administrative assistant	
42. Ted Uyematsu	early 20s	single	law student	
43. Jenny Kato**	early 20s	single	teacher	
44. Stan Hifumi	late 30s	single	attorney	brother of #45
45. Sandi Okawa	late 40s	married	substitute teacher	sister of #44
46. Terry Winters	late30s	married (white)	medical supply distributor	
47. Laura Nee	late 30s	single	professional fundraiser	
48. Dani Murayama	late 20s	single	pediatrics coordinator	daughter of #49
49. Linda Murayama	early 50s	single	school director	mother of #48
50. Bill Saito	late 20s	single	school principal	
51. Marilyn Tokubo	late 20s	single	insurance	
52. Diane Okihiro	mid 20s	single	retail sales	
53. Kristi Kamamura	late 20s	single	pediatrics coordinator	
54. Carol Wong	early 50s	married	dietician	
55. Dale Kawachi	mid 30s	single	banking	

Name	Age Category	Marital Status	Occupation	Family Relation
56. Fred Yang	mid 40s	married (white)	computer programmer	
57. Jeremy Shih	mid 70s	married	chemist (retired)	
58. Cathy Leong	early 30s	married (Japanese)	financial analyst	
59. David Masuda	late 20s	single	physical therapist	
60. Lynn Jong	mid 40s	single	administrator	
61. Philip Fukuda	early 20s	single	actor	
62. Victor Ong	early 50s	married (white)	film-maker	
63. Paula Inouye	mid 40s	single	kitchen designer	
64. Rob Yamaguchi	early 30s	married	program analyst	
65. Tracy Nagata	mid 20s	single	graduate student	
66. Beth Chang	late 40s	married (white)	health technician	
67. Cindy Baker	late 30s	married (white)	administrator	
68. Brad Ow	early 30s	married (white)	attorney	
69. Nathan Yang	late 30s	single	landscape design	
70. George Hsieh	early 40s	married (Japanese)	cardiologist	
71. Michael Lowe	late 20s	single	pharmaceutical sales	
72. Kelly Sung	late 20s	single	pharmacist	
73. Randall Tom	early 30s	single	graduate student	
74. Andy Kawachi	mid 40s	married (white)	UPS delivery person	
75. Russ Chu	late 30s	single	stock broker	
76. Karen Flores	late 30s	married (Latino)	customer relations	cousin of #77
77. Dawn Chin	late 30s	married (Japanese)	teacher	cousin of #76
78. Audry Mah	late 60s	widowed	school principal (retired)	
79. Cathy Choy	late 20s	single	accountant	
80. Steve Fukuda	late 40s	married	pharmacist	spouse of #81
81. Ellen Fukuda	late 40s	married	teacher's aide	spouse of #80
82. Sam Kang	late 20s	single	engineer	
83. Rose Kogawa	early 40s	married (Chinese)	airline agent and musician	spouse of #84
84. Bob Cheng	mid 40s	married (Japanese)	sales accountant	spouse of #83
85. Roger Lo	early 40s	single	professor	brother of #86
86. Sara Lo	late 40s	single	physician	sister of #85
87. Chuck Hayashi	late 40s	married	high school counselor	
88. Joy Matsui	mid 40s	married	receptionist	
89. Marjorie Aoki	late 40s	married	teacher	spouse of #90
90. John Aoki	mid 50s	married	accountant	spouse of #89

Name	Age Category	Marital Status	Occupation	Family Relation
91. Ken Mineta	early 50s	married	pharmacist	spouse of #92
92. Susan Mineta	early 50s	married	medical technologist	spouse of #91
93. Kanji Furuye	mid 40s	married	computer programmer	
94. Dale Fujimoto	late 40s	married	accountant	
95. Barry Sato	early 40s	single	publisher	

*All names have been changed to ensure anonymity.
** A person is of mixed Chinese-Japanese ancestry.
NOTE: Parentheses in marital status column indicate intermarried individuals and the race/ethnicity of the spouse.

NOTES 🔲

CHAPTER 1 *Introduction*

1. Senator D'Amato apologizes for faking Japanese accent, *San Francisco Chronicle*, 6 April 1995, p. A2; Emile Guillermo, D'Amato's actions were worse than a slur, *San Francisco Chronicle*, 7 April 1995, p. A27; Melinda Henneberger, D'Amato gives a new apology on Ito remarks, *New York Times*, 8 April 1995, p. A1; Stewart Kwoh and Julie Su, Individuals lose when a group is demeaned, *Los Angeles Times*, 25 April 1995, p. B13.
2. Senator D'Amato apologizes, A2.
3. Los Angeles Police Captain Margaret York.
4. All of the interviewers were of Asian descent (Chinese, Japanese, Filipino, Thai), and all but one were U.C.L.A. undergraduates; the exception was a recent graduate of U.C. Berkeley who assisted with interviews conducted in the San Francisco Bay area.

CHAPTER 2 *Racialized Ethnics Compared to White Ethnics*

1. To be sure, "whiteness" as a color in and of itself has gained attention in recent years in both academic and lay circles (see Frankenberg, 1993; Gallagher, 1995; Ignatiev, 1995; Roediger, 1991). Charges of reverse discrimination against the typical "white male" based on affirmative action policies and other minority set-aside programs are at the forefront of such debates and reflect the increasing politicization of race.
2. Warner and Srole (1945), authors of one of the classic studies of assimilation, represent an important exception. They are quite clear in stating that race profoundly complicates standard understandings of assimilation processes.
3. Of course, this answer does not satisfactorily explain why racial minority groups who immigrated at roughly the same historical moment and time as European immigrants were not accepted as readily as their European counterparts. Nor does this answer satisfactorily explain how forced enslavement (as in the case of Africans) or incorporation (as

in the case of Mexicans and Native Americans) complicates the assimilation process.

4. Stephen G. Graubard, Why do Asian pupils win those prizes?, *New York Times*, January 29, 1988, p.A35.

5. Robert B. Oxnam, Why Asians succeed here, *New York Times Magazine*, 30 November 1986, p. 70.

6. *Newsweek*, 6 December 1982, pp. 39–51.

7. These "whitening" processes are both literal and metaphorical. In the literal sense, they refer to the high intermarriage rates between Asian-Americans and white Americans. Metaphorically, great emphasis has been placed on the "fit" between Confucianism and the Protestant work ethic (see Stephen Graubard, Why do Asian pupils win those prizes?, *New York Times*, 29 January 1988, p. A35; Robert B. Oxnam, Why Asians succeed here, *New York Times Magazine*, 30 November 1986, p. 70; Asian-Americans: A 'model' minority, *Newsweek*, 6 December 1982, p.39–51.

8. Available statistics for Asian-Americans do not provide detailed information on generational status; distinctions are drawn only between the native and foreign born. This limitation should be kept in mind in the following discussion since the category, native born, lumps various generations together.

9. This category includes Chinese, East Indian, Japanese, Korean, Filipino, Pacific Islander, and the category "other Asian." It excludes Asian students with International or Foreign status.

10. Steven Holmes, Census sees a profound ethnic shift in U. S., *New York Times*, 14 March 1996, p.A8; Steven Holmes, Black-white marriages on rise, study says, *New York Times*, 4 July 1996, p.A10; Steven Holmes, Census tests category to identify racial groups, *New York Times*, 6 December 1996, p.A1; Linda Mathews, More than identity rides on a new racial category, *New York Times*, 9 July 1996, p.A1; Michael Marriott, Multiracial Americans ready to claim their identity, *New York Times*, 20 July 1996, p.A1.

11. A recent article by Alethea Yip in *Asian Week* represents an important exception. Pan-Asian bonds of matrimony, 14 February 1997, p.12.

12. As Fong (1982), Kitano and Daniels (1988), Nishi (1989), Takaki (1987, 1989b), and Wei (1993) point out, Asian ethnics historically have needed to prove the legitimacy of their status as "real" Americans and endure the question, "Where are you *really* from?"

13. In response to the rapid increase in Asian-American student enrollment, white students humorously claimed that M.I.T. stood for Made in Taiwan and that U.C.L.A. stood for University of Caucasians Living Among Asians (Osajima, 1988; Takagi, 1992).

14. Quoted in Alan Elsner, Asian-Americans feel victimized by fund-raising scandal, Reuters News Service, 8 August 1997.

15. Quoted in Stacy Lavilla, What Asian-Americans make, *Asian Week*, March 5, 1998, p.16.

16. What Asian-Americans make, p.16.

CHAPTER 3 *Cars, Girls, and Baseball—but with an Asian Twist*

1. All names have been changed to protect the anonymity of our respondents.
2. Throughout this book, I refer to the terms *Sansei* and *Yonsei* to describe the generational status of Japanese-Americans. Sansei denotes third-generation status, and Yonsei denotes fourth-generation status.
3. The three exceptions are all of Chinese-Japanese ancestry. They are Tony Lam, Emily Woo, and Jenny Kato. Today, the situation is rapidly changing as more intermarriages take place and more biracial/multiracial and biethnic/multiethnic children are born. How their children will be socialized ethnically and whether they will identify with one, a combination, or none of their ancestries is not clear. A budding literature is now emerging to take into account this rapidly growing trend and its consequences for Asian-American ethnic identity (Mass, 1992; Root, 1996; Standen, 1996; Williams, 1992).
4. California did not repeal its laws against miscegenation until 1948. As late as 1967, when the Supreme Court ruled all miscegenation laws invalid, sixteen states still prohibited mixed-race marriages.

CHAPTER 4 *"I knew I was different"*

1. Typical communities that were mentioned include: Sacramento, San Diego, Anaheim, Long Beach, Orinda, Fresno, Whittier, Agoura Hills, San Dimas, Hayward, and Walnut Creek. The remainder of the respondents grew up in states such as Oregon, Illinois, and Texas.
2. The exceptions were respondents who attended Buddhist churches and youth groups—a small handful who were more likely to stress the cultural learning that took place.
3. Upscale Asian-American bedroom communities have emerged in the last few decades, particularly in the Los Angeles area. Today, aspiring Asian-American families can move into an Asian centered suburban community if they so choose. Monterey Park, for example, has been touted as the first "suburban Chinatown" as well as the Chinese-American Beverly Hills and has successfully attracted upwardly mobile Asian-American families, both foreign and American born (Fong, 1994; Horton, 1995). Today, more than half of the community's population are Asian-Americans of varying ethnicities. Communities such as Monterey Park present an interesting challenge to the premise that suburbanization necessarily reduces ties to one's ethnic group (Cohen, 1977).
4. See Saito (1993) for an excellent discussion of the history of relations between the Japanese and Chinese in Monterey Park.

CHAPTER 5 *"Practicality always steps in"*

1. See Okamura's (1981) paper on "situational ethnicity" for a discussion on the shifting levels of ethnic identities depending on the context of interaction.
2. Of the thirty-seven respondents who are parents, about one- third have adolescent children; the remainder have college-age or older children.

BIBLIOGRAPHY

Alba, R. (Ed). (1985a). *Ethnicity and race in the U.S.A.: Toward the twenty-first century.* London: Routledge & Kegan Paul.

———. (1985b). The twilight of ethnicity among Americans of European ancestry: The case of Italians. In R. Alba (Ed.), *Ethnicity and race in the U.S.A.: Toward the twenty-first century* (pp. 134–158). London: Routledge & Kegan Paul.

———. (1990). *Ethnicity in America: The transformation of white America.* New Haven, CT: Yale University Press.

———. (1995). Assimilation's quiet tide. *Public Interest 119,* 3–18.

Alba, R., & Chamlin, M. B. (1983). A preliminary examination of ethnic identification among whites. *American Sociological Review 48,* 240–247.

Alba, R., & Nee, V. (1996, January). *The Assimilation of Immigrant Groups: Concept, Theory and Evidence.* Paper presented at the conference on becoming American/America becoming: International migration to the United States, Social Science Research Council.

Allen, T. W. (1994). *The invention of the white race.* London: Verso.

Almaguer, T. (1994). *Racial fault lines: The historical origins of white supremacy in California.* Berkeley: University of California Press.

Ancheta, A. (1998). *Race, rights, and the Asian-American experience.* New Brunswick, NJ: Rutgers University Press.

Attacks against Asian-Americans are rising (1995, December 13). *New York Times,* p. A16.

Barrera, M. (1979). *Race and class in the southwest.* Notre Dame, IN: University of Notre Dame Press.

Barringer, H. R., Gardner, R. W., & Levin, M. J. (1993). *Asian and Pacific islanders in the United States.* New York: Russell Sage Foundation.

Barringer, H. R., Takeuchi, D. T., & Xenos, P. (1990). Education, occupational prestige, and income of Asian-Americans. *Sociology of Education 63,* 27–43.

Bell, D. (1992). *Faces at the bottom of the well.* New York: Basic Books.

Bell, D. A. (1985, July 15). The triumph of Asian-Americans. *The New Republic 22,* 24–31.

Benjamin, L. (1991). *The black elite: Facing the color line in the twilight of the twentieth century.* Chicago: Nelson-Hall Publishers.

Bershtel, S., & Graubard, A. (1992). *Saving remnants.* Berkeley: University of California Press.

Blauner, R. (1972). *Racial oppression in America.* New York: Harper & Row.

Blumer, H. (1958). Race prejudice as a sense of group position. *Pacific Sociological Review 1,* 3–7.

Bodnar, J. (1992). *Remaking America: Public memory, commemoration, and patriotism in the twentieth century.* Princeton, NJ: Princeton University Press.

Broom, L., & Kitsuse, J. I. (1955). The validation of acculturation: A condition of ethnic assimilation. *American Anthropologist 57,*44–48.

Burawoy, M., et al. (1991). *Ethnography unbound: Power and resistance in the modern metropolis.* Berkeley: University of California Press.

Chan, K., & Hune, S. (1995). Racialization and panethnicity: From Asians in America to Asian-Americans. In W. Hawley and A. Jackson (Eds.), *Toward a common destiny: Race and ethnic relations in American schools* (pp. 205–233). San Francisco: Jossey-Bass.

Chan, S. (1991a). The exclusion of Chinese women, 1870–1943. In Sucheng Chan (Ed.), *Entry denied: Exclusion and the Chinese community in America, 1882–1943* (pp. 94–146). Philadelphia: Temple University Press.

———. (1991b). *Asian-Americans: An interpretive history.* Boston: Twayne Publishers.

Chavez, L. (1991). *Out of the barrio: Toward a new politics of Hispanic assimilation.* New York: Basic Books.

Chin, D. (1994, August 1). Unspoiled Asian woman? Bah! *Los Angeles Times,* p. B11.

Cohen, S. (1977). Socioeconomic determinants of intraethnic marriage and friendship. *Social Forces 55*(4), 997–1010.

Collins, S. (1997). *Black corporate executives: The making and breaking of a black middle class.* Philadelphia: Temple University Press.

Commission on Wartime Relocation and Internment of Civilians (CWRIC). (1982). *Personal Justice Denied.* Washington, DC: U.S. Government Printing Office.

Cose, E. (1993). *The rage of a privileged class.* New York: HarperCollins.

Crispino, J. A. (1980). *The assimilation of ethnic groups: The Italian case.* New York: Center for Migration Studies.

Daniels, R. (1972). *Concentration camps U.S.A.: Japanese-Americans and World War II.* New York: Holt, Rinehart and Winston, Inc.

———. (1988). *Asian America: Chinese and Japanese in the United States since 1850.* Seattle: University of Washington Press.

———. (1991). *Japanese-Americans: From relocation to redress.* Seattle: University of Washington Press.

Der, H. (1993). Asian Pacific Islanders and the 'glass ceiling': New era of civil rights activism? In LEAP Asian Pacific American Public Policy Institute (Eds.), *The state of Asian Pacific America: Policy issues to the year 2020* (pp. 215–231). Los Angeles: The Editors.

Divorky, D. (1988). The model minority goes to school. *Phi Delta Kappan 70*(3), 219–222.

Early, G. (1993). *Lure and loathing: Essays on race, identity, and the ambivalence of assimilation.* New York: Allen Lane, The Penguin Press.

Espiritu, Y. L. (1992). *Asian-American panethnicity.* Philadelphia: Temple University Press.

————. (1994). The intersection of race, ethnicity, and class: The multiple identities of second-generation Filipinos. *Ethnicity 1*, 249–273.

Fawcett, J. T., & Cariño, B. V. (Eds). (1987). *Pacific bridges: The new immigration from Asia and the Pacific Islands.* New York: Center for Migration Studies.

Feagin, J., & Sikes, M. (1994). *Living with racism: The black middle-class experience.* Boston: Beacon Press.

The 50 most beautiful people in the world. *People Magazine* [online]. HTTP:http://pathfinder.com/people/980223/skaters/Nancy4.html (1998, February 23).

Fong, C., & Yung, J. (1995). In search of the right spouse. *Amerasia Journal 21*(3), 77–98.

Fong, D. (1982, May 1). America's invisible Chinese. *New York Times*, p. A27.

Fong, T. (1998). *Contemporary Asian-American experience.* Englewood Cliffs, NJ: Prentice-Hall.

Fordham, S. (1997). *Blacked out.* Chicago: University of Chicago Press.

Frankenberg, R. (1993). *White women, race matters: The social construction of whiteness.* Minneapolis: University of Minnesota Press.

Fugita, S., & O'Brien, D. J. (1991a). *Japanese-American ethnicity: The persistence of community.* Seattle: University of Washington Press.

————. (1991b). *The Japanese-American experience.* Bloomington: Indiana University Press.

Gans, H. (1979). Symbolic ethnicity: The future of ethnic groups and cultures in America. *Ethnic and Racial Studies 2*, 1–19.

Glazer, N. (1993). Is assimilation dead? *Annals of the American Academy of Political and Social Science, 530*, 122–136.

Glazer, N., & Moynihan, D. (1975). *Beyond the melting pot.* Cambridge: M.I.T. Press.

Gold, S., & Nazli K. (1993). Vietnamese refugees and blocked mobility. *Asian and Pacific Migration Journal 2*(1), 27–55.

Goldberg, G. (1970). *East meets west: The story of the Chinese and Japanese in California.* New York: Harcourt Brace Jovanovich.

Gordon, M. (1964). *Assimilation in American life.* New York: Oxford University Press.

Greeley, A. (1971). *Why can't they be like us: America's white ethnic groups.* New York: E. P. Dutton.

————. (1974). *Ethnicity in the United States: A preliminary reconnaissance.* New York: Wiley.

Guillermo, E. (1997, August 22). Many forms of bashing. *Asian Weekly*, p. 5.

Hacker, A. (1992). *Two nations.* New York: Scribner's.

Hamamoto, D. (1994). *Monitored peril: Asian-Americans and the politics of television representation.* Minneapolis: University of Minnesota Press.

Haney-Lopez, I. (1996). *White by law*. New York: New York University Press.

Hansen, M. (1938). *The problem of the third-generation immigrant*. Rock Island, IL: Augustana Historical Society.

Hayano, D. M. (1981). Ethnic identification and disidentification: Japanese-American views of Chinese-Americans. *Ethnic Groups 3*, 157–171.

Higham, J. (1963). *Strangers in the land*. New Brunswick, NJ: Rutgers University Press.

Hing, B. O. (1993). *Making and remaking Asian-America through immigration policy, 1850–1990*. Stanford: Stanford University Press.

Hirschman, C. (1983). America's melting pot reconsidered. *Annual Review of Sociology 9*, 397–423.

Hirschman, C., & Wong, M. G. (1981). Trends in socioeconomic achievement among immigrant and native-born Asian-Americans. *Sociological Quarterly 22*, 495–513.

Horsman, R. (1981). *Race and manifest destiny*. Cambridge: Harvard University Press.

Horton, J. (1995). *The politics of diversity: immigration, resistance, and change in Monterey Park, California*. Philadelphia: Temple University Press.

Hosokawa, F. (1978). *The Sansei: Social interaction and ethnic identification among the third-generation Japanese*. San Francisco: R & E Research Associations, Inc.

Huhr, W. M., & Kim, K. C. (1989). Success image of Asian-Americans: Its validity and its practical and theoretical implications. *Ethnic and Racial Studies 12*, 512–538.

Ignatiev, N. (1995). *How the Irish became white*. New York: Routledge.

Jiobu, R. M. (1988). *Ethnicity & assimilation: Blacks, Chinese, Filipinos, Japanese, Koreans, Mexicans, Vietnamese, and Whites*. Albany: State University of New York Press.

Kellogg, S. (1990). Exploring diversity in middle-class families: The symbolism of American ethnic identity. *Social Science History 14*(1), 27–41.

Kendis, K. O. (1989). *A matter of comfort: Ethnic maintenance and ethnic style among third-generation Japanese-Americans*. New York: AMS Press, Inc.

Kim, E. (1986). Asian-American and American popular culture. In *Dictionary of Asian-American history* (pp. 99–114). Chicago: University of Chicago Press.

King, R. (1997). Multiraciality reigns supreme? *Amerasia Journal 23*(1), 113–128.

King, R., & Da Costa, K. M. (1996). Changing face, changing race. In M. Root (Ed.), *Multiracial experience* (pp. 227–244). Thousand Oaks, CA: Sage Publications.

Kitano, H.H.L. (1992). *Generations and identity: The Japanese-American*. Needham Heights, MA: Ginn Press.

Kitano, H.H.L., & Daniels, R. (1995). *Asian-Americans: Emerging minorities*. Englewood Cliffs, NJ: Prentice-Hall.

Kitano, H.H.L., Yeung, W., Chai, L., & Hatanaka, H. (1984). Asian-American interracial marriage. *Journal of Marriage and the Family 46*(1), 179–190.

Kristol, I. (1972). The Negro today is like the immigrant of yesterday. In P. I. Rose (Ed.), *Nation of nations: The ethnic experience and the racial crisis* (pp. 197–210). New York: Random House.

LaFromboise, T., Coleman, H.L.K., & Gerton, J. (1993). Psychological impact of biculturalism: Evidence and theory. *Psychological Bulletin 114*, 395–412.

Landry, B. (1987). *The new black middle class*. Berkeley: University of California Press.

LEAP Asian Pacific American Public Policy Institute & UCLA Asian-American Studies Center (Eds.). (1993). *The state of Asian Pacific America: Policy issues to the year 2020*. Los Angeles: The Editors.

Lee, S. (1996). *Unraveling the "model minority" stereotype: Listening to Asian-American youth*. New York: Teachers College Press.

Lee, S. M. (1989). Asian immigration and American race relations: From exclusion to acceptance? *Ethnic and Racial Studies 12*(3), 368–390.

Lee, S. M., & Yamanaka, K. (1990). Patterns of Asian-American intermarriage and marital assimilation, *Journal Of Comparative Family Studies 21*(2), 287–305.

Lieberson, S. (1981). *A piece of the pie: Black and white immigrants since 1880*. Berkeley: University of California Press.

———. (1985). Unhyphenated whites in the United States. In Richard D. Alba (Ed.), *Ethnicity and race in the U.S.A.: Toward the twenty-first century* (pp. 159–180). London: Routledge & Kegan Paul.

Lieberson, S., & Waters, M. (1988). *From many strands*. New York: Russell Sage Foundation.

Loewen, J. W. (1971). *The Mississippi Chinese: Between black and white*. Cambridge: Harvard University Press.

Lorde, A. (1984). *Sister outsider: Essays and speeches*. Trumansburg, NY: Crossing Press.

Lowe, L. (1996). *Immigrant acts*. Durham, NC: Duke University Press.

Louis, K. K. (1931). A study of American-born and American-reared Chinese in Los Angeles. Ph.D. dissertation, University of California, Berkeley.

Lyman, S. (1986). Chinatown and Little Tokyo: Power, conflict, and community among Chinese and Japanese immigrants in America. Millwood, NY: Associated Faculty Press.

McBee, S. (1984, April 2). Asian-Americans: Are they making the grade? *U.S. News and World Report 96*(B), 41–47.

McIntosh, P. (1997). White privilege: Unpacking the invisible knapsack, in Bart Schneider (Ed.), *Race: An Anthology in the first person* (pp.120–126). New York: Three Rivers Press.

Magiera, M. (1992). Yamaguchi hot to endorse clothes, cars. *Advertising Age 63*(12), 10.

Mass, A. (1992). Interracial Japanese-Americans: The best of both worlds or the end of the Japanese-American community? In M. Root (Ed.), *Racially mixed people in America* (pp. 265–279). Newbury Park, CA: Sage Publications.

Massey, D. S., & Denton, N. (1987). Trends in the residential segregation of Blacks, Hispanics, and Asians. *American Sociological Review 52*, 802–825.

Matusow, B. (1989). Alone together. *Washingtonian 25*(2), 153–290.

Maykovitch, M. (1972). *Japanese-American identity dilemma.* Tokyo: Waseda University Press.

Min, P. G. (1995). Major issues relating to Asian-American experiences. In P. G. Min (Ed.), *Asian-Americans: Contemporary trends and issues* (pp. 38–57). Thousand Oaks, CA.: Sage.

Mittleberg, D., & Waters, M. (1992) The process of enthogenesis among Haitian and Israeli immigrants in the United States. *Ethnic and Racial Studies 15*(3), 412–435

Montero, D. (1980). *Japanese-Americans: Changing patterns of ethnic affiliation over three generations.* Boulder, CO: Westview Press.

Moore, M. (1988). Scapegoats again. *Progressive 52*, 25–28.

Murray, C. (1994). Affirmative racism. In N. Mills (Ed.), *Debating affirmative action* (pp. 191–208). New York: Bantam Doubleday.

Nagata, D. (1993). *Legacy of injustice: Exploring the cross-generational impact of the Japanese-American internment.* New York: Plenum Press.

Nagel, J. 1991. The political construction of ethnicity. In N. R. Yetman (Ed.), *Majority and minority: The dynamics of race and ethnicity in American life* (pp. 76–86). Boston: Allyn and Bacon.

———. 1994. Constructing ethnicity: Creating and recreating ethnic identity and culture. *Social Problems 41*, 152–176.

———. (1995). American Indian ethnic renewal: Politics and the resurgence of identity. *American Sociological Review 60*, 947–965.

National Asian Pacific American Legal Consortium (NAPALC). (1997). *1996 audit of violence against Asian Pacific Americans.* Washington DC: NAPALC.

Nee, V., & Sanders, J. (1985). The road to parity: Determinants of the socioeconomic achievements of Asian-Americans. *Ethnic and Racial Studies 8*, 75–93.

Nee, V., & Wong, H. Y. (1985). Asian-American socioeconomic achievement: The strength of the family bond. *Sociological Perspectives 28*, 281–306.

Nishi, S. M. (1989). Perceptions and deceptions: Contemporary views of Asian-Americans. In Grace Yun (Ed.), *A look beyond the model minority image: Critical issues in Asian America* (pp. 3–10). New York: Minority Rights Group, Inc.

Noble, K. B. (1995, December 13). Attacks against Asian-Americans are rising. *New York Times*, p. A16.

Novak, M. (1973). *The rise of the unmeltable ethnics.* New York: Macmillan.

Okihiro, G. (1994). *Margins and mainstreams: Asians in American history and culture.* Seattle: University of Washington Press.

Omi, M. (1993). Out of the melting pot and into the fire: Race relations policy. In LEAP Asian Pacific American Public Policy Institute & U.C.L.A. Asian-American Studies Center (Eds.), *The state of Asian*

Pacific America: policy issues to the year 2020 (pp. 199–214). Los Angeles: The Editors.

Omi, M., & Winant, H. (1994). *Racial formation in the United States.* New York: Routledge.

Onishi, N. (1996, May 30). New sense of race arises among Asian-Americans. *New York Times,* p. A1.

Osajima, K. (1988). Asian-Americans as the model minority: An analysis of the popular press image in the 1960s and 1980s. In G. Y. Okihiro, S. Hune, A. A. Hansen, & J. M. Liu (Eds.), *Reflections on shattered windows: Promises and prospects for Asian-American studies* (pp. 81–91). Pullman: Washington State University Press.

———. (1993). The hidden injuries of race. In L. Revilla, G. Nomura, S. Wong, & S. Hune (Eds.), *Bearing dreams and shaping visions.* Pullman: Washington State University Press.

Park, R. (1950). *Race and culture: Essays in the sociology of contemporary man.* Chicago: University of Chicago Press.

Park, R., & Burgess, E. (1921). *Introduction to the science of sociology.* Chicago: University of Chicago Press.

Petersen, W. (1966, January 6). Success story, Japanese-American style. *The New York Times Magazine,* p. 20.

———. (1972). *Japanese-Americans.* New York: Random House.

Phinney, J. S. (1990). Ethnic identity in adolescents and adults: Review of research. *Psychological Bulletin 108,* 499–514.

Pimental, B. (1995, August 1). Violence up sharply against U.S. Asians: Study finds 35 percent rise in '94. *San Francisco Chronicle,* p. A3.

Powell, J. (1997). Are you going to the march? In B. Schneider (Ed.), *Race: An anthology in the first person* (pp. 112–117). New York: Three Rivers Press.

Robinson, R. (1998). *Defending the spirit: A black life in America.* New York: E. P. Dutton.

Roediger, D. R. (1991). *The wages of whiteness: Race and the making of the American working class.* New York: Verso.

Root, M. (Ed.). (1992). *Racially mixed people in America.* Newbury Park, CA: Sage.

Rose, P. (1985). Asian-Americans: From pariahs to paragons. In N. Glazer (Ed.), *Clamor at the gates: The new American immigration* (pp. 181–212). San Francisco: Institute for Contemporary Studies.

Said, E. (1979). *Orientalism.* New York: Vintage Books.

Saito, L. (1993). Contrasting patterns of adaptation: Japanese-Americans and Chinese immigrants in Monterey Park. In L. Revilla, G. Nomura, S. Wong, & S. Hune (Eds.), *Bearing dreams and shaping visions: Asian Pacific American perspectives* (pp. 33–43). Pullman: Washington State University Press.

Shinagawa, L. H., & Pang, G. Y. (1996). Asian-American panethnicity and intermarriage. *Amerasia Journal 22*(2), 127–132.

Sowell, T. (1981). *Ethnic America.* New York: Basic Books.

Spencer, P. (1996, Dec./Jan). The power of traditions. *Parenting,* 167–172.

Spickard, P. (1989). *Mixed blood: Intermarriage and ethnic identity in twentieth-century America.* Madison: University of Wisconsin Press.

Standen, B. (1996). Without a template: The biracial Korean/white experience. In M. Root (Ed.), *The multiracial experience*, (pp. 245–262). Newbury Park, CA: Sage.

Stanfield, J. H. II (1993). Epistemological considerations: Race and ethnicity in research methods. In J. H. Stanfield II & R. M. Dennis (Eds.), *Race and ethnicity in research methods* (pp. 16–36). Newbury Park, CA: Sage.

Steinberg, S. (1989). *The ethnic myth: Race, ethnicity, and class in America*. Boston: Beacon Press.

Stevens, G. (1992). The social and demographic context of language use in the United States. *American Sociological Review 50*, 74–83.

Sue, S., & Okazaki, S. (1990). Asian-American educational achievements: A phenomenon in search of an explanation. *American Psychologist 45*(8), 913–920.

Sung, B. L. (1990). *Chinese American intermarriage*. New York: Center for Migration Studies.

Suzuki, B. (1977). Education and the socialization of Asian-Americans: A revisionist analysis of the model minority thesis. *Amerasia 4*, 23–51.

———. (1989). Asian-Americans as the 'model minority.' *Change 21*, 13–19.

Swift, E. M. (1992). All that glitters. *Sports Illustrated 77*(25), 70.

Takagi, D. Y. (1992). *The retreat from race: Asian-American admissions and racial politics*. New Brunswick, NJ: Rutgers University Press.

Takaki, R. (1987). *From different shores*. New York: Oxford University Press.

———. (1989a). Who killed Vincent Chin? In Grace Yun (Ed.), *A look beyond the model minority image: Critical issues in Asian America* (pp. 23–29). New York: Minority Rights Group, Inc.

———. (1989b). *Strangers from a different shore*. New York: Penguin Books.

———. (1993). *A different mirror: A history of multicultural America*. Boston: Little, Brown and Company.

Tinker, J. N. (1982). Intermarriage and assimilation in a plural society: Japanese-Americans in the United States. *Marriage and Family Review 5*, 61–74.

Uba, L. (1994). *Asian-Americans: Personality patterns, identity, and mental health*. New York: Guilford Press.

U.S. Bureau of the Census. (1993a). *1990 census of population: Asians and Pacific Islanders in the United States*. CP–3–5. Washington, DC.

———. (1993b). *1990 census of population: Social and economic characteristics, California*. Section 1. CP–2–6. Washington, DC.

U.S. Commission on Civil Rights. (1986). *Recent activities against citizens and residents of Asian Ancestry*. Washington, DC: Government Printing Office.

———. (1992). *Civil rights issues facing Asian-Americans, 1990*. Washington, DC: Government Printing Office.

Veltman, Calvin. (1983). *Language shift in the United States*. Berlin: Mouton.

Vo, L. (1996). Asian immigrants, Asian-Americans, and the politics of ethnic mobilization in San Diego. *Amerasia Journal 22*(2), 89–108.

Walton, A. (1989, August 20). Willie Horton and me. *New York Times Magazine*, p. 52.

Warren, J., & Twine, F. (1994). We the people and blacks: Whitening North American style. Unpublished manuscript.

Warner, W. L., & Srole, L. (1945). *The social systems of American ethnic groups.* New Haven, CT: Yale University Press.

Waters, M. C. (1986). The process and content of ethnic identification: A study of white ethnics in suburbia. Ph.D. dissertation, .

———. (1990). *Ethnic options: Choosing identities in America.* Berkeley: University of California Press.

———. (1992). The construction of a symbolic ethnicity: Suburban white ethnics in the 1980s. In M. D'Innocenzo & J. P. Sirefman (Eds.), *Immigration and Ethnicity: American society—'melting pot' or 'salad bowl'?* (pp. 75–90). Westport, CT: Greenwood Press.

Wei, W. (1993). *The Asian-American movement.* Philadelphia: Temple University Press.

Weiss, M. S. (1973). Selective acculturation and the dating Process. In S. Sue & N. N. Wagner (Eds.), *Asian-Americans: Psychological perspectives.* Palo Alto: Science and Behavior Books.

West, C. (1993). *Race matters.* Boston: Beacon Press.

White, M. J., Biddlecom, A. E., & Guo, S. (1993). Immigration, naturalization, and residential assimilation among Asian-Americans in 1980. *Social Forces 72*(1), 93–117.

Wilson, W. J. (1978). *The declining significance of race.* Chicago: University of Chicago Press.

Williams, T. (1992). Prism lives: Identity of binational Amerasians. In M. Root (Ed.) *Racially mixed people in America* (pp. 265–279). Newbury Park, CA: Sage.

Wong, B. P. (1982). *Chinatown: Economic adaptation and ethnic identity of the Chinese.* New York: Holt, Rinehart and Winston.

Wong, M. G. (1989). A look at intermarriage among the Chinese in the United States. *Sociological Perspectives 32*,87–107.

———. (1995). Chinese-Americans. In Pyong Gap Min (Ed.), *Asian-Americans: Contemporary trends and issues* (pp. 58–94). Thousand Oaks, CA: Sage.

Wu, D.T.L. (1997). *Asian Pacific Americans in the workplace.* Walnut Creek, CA: AltaMira Press.

Yancey, W. L., Ericksen, E. P., & Juliani, R. N. (1976). Emergent ethnicity: A review and reformulation. *American Sociological Review 41*, 391–403.

Yasutake, S. (1977). *Japanese-American experience of Nisei parents and their children and implications for education.* Ann Arbor, MI: University Microfilms International.

Yun, G. (Ed.) (1989). *A look beyond the model minority image: Critical issues in Asian America.* New York: Minority Rights Group, Inc.

Zack, N. (1992). *Race and mixed race.* Philadelphia: Temple University Press.

———. (1995). *American mixed race: The culture of microdiversity.* Lanham, MD: Rowman & Littlefield.

———. (Ed.) (1996). *The Multiracial experience*. Thousand Oaks, CA: Sage.

Zenner, W. P. (1985). Jewishness in America: Ascription and choice. In R. D. Alba (Ed.), *Ethnicity and race in the U.S.A.: Toward the twenty-first century*. London: Routledge & Kegan Paul.

Zia, H., & Gall, S. B. (Eds.) (1995). *Notable Asian-Americans*. New York: Gale Research.

Zinn, L. (1992, March 9). To marketers, Kristi Yamaguchi isn't as good as gold. *Business Week 3255*, 40.

INDEX

ABOUT THE AUTHOR

Mia Tuan is an assistant professor of sociology at the University of Oregon. She received her B.A. degree from the University of California at Berkeley and her Ph.D. from the University of California at Los Angeles. In addition to racial and ethnic identity development among multigeneration Asian-Americans, her research interests include immigrant adaptation and identity issues facing cross-racial adoptees.